SQ

Dear Steve and Siobhan,

Thanks for all you are to Penny and myself. Without you, we wouldn't be able to do what we're doing — you're our armour-bearers and great ones at that!

We _so_ appreciate you,

Love
Dan
June '03

All enquiries regarding this publication
and Dave Gilpin's speaking engagements to be made to:

V3 Leadership
The Megacentre
Sheffield
S2 5BQ
United Kingdom

Tel: +44 (0)114 272 5077
E-mail: info@v3leadership.com
www.v3leadership.com
Information and resources can be found at
www.hopecity.co.uk

SQ

How to Increase Your Spiritual IQ

Dave Gilpin

Monarch
BOOKS

Mill Hill, London & Grand Rapids, Michigan

First published by Monarch Books in the UK in 2003,
Concorde House, Grenville Place,
Mill Hill, London, NW7 3SA.

Illustrations by Bridget Gillespie

Distributed by:
UK: STL, PO Box 300, Kingstown Broadway, Carlisle,
Cumbria CA3 0QS;
USA: Kregel Publications, PO Box 2607,
Grand Rapids, Michigan 49501.

ISBN 1 85424 617 8 (UK)
ISBN 0 8254 6222 3 (USA)

British Library Cataloguing Data
A catalogue record for this book is available
from the British Library.

Book design and production for the publishers by
Bookprint Creative Services
P.O. Box 827, BN21 3YJ, England.
Printed in Great Britain.

DEDICATION

To a very special young man
with a very great future:
Ryan

To one who carried a pioneer
spirit that now lives in his son:
Dr Alan Gilpin

CONTENTS

WHAT THEY'RE SAYING ABOUT SQ

A very well structured handbook to spirituality which should be a challenge to all who read it.

Fiona Castle
TV personality

Angelo Dundee coined the phrase "float like a butterfly, sting like a bee" to describe Muhammad Ali. Dave Gilpin's writing reminds me of that. His deft footwork, artistry and lightness of touch, combined with a powerful knockout punch, make this manual in the art of living a joy to read and a powerful resource. Don't buy it if you don't want to be encouraged, challenged and empowered, because it will do all of that and more.

Rev. Eric Delve
Area Dean of Maidstone, Six Preacher of Canterbury Cathedral

Dave Gilpin has produced a clever and convincing book. It is a brilliant challenge to many of the popular clichés and misconceptions that all too often limit people or reduce their potential. Faith and humour run through every page. These are powerful combinations and have the capacity to radically change mindsets. It is more powerful because he has personally worked these issues out in his own experience.

Dr David Cartledge
President of Southern Cross College of the Assemblies of God, Australia, and a member of the Australian Assemblies of God National Executive

David Gilpin challenges the status quo and inspires others to find a larger horizon, dream bigger dreams and attempt the impossible. Using well-known phrases, he develops many godly principles which, applied to your life, will make you a better person.

David Shearman
Senior Minister of Christian Centre, Nottingham, England

This book is refreshingly different. It is full of wisdom and insight from an author who is a prophetic leader to this generation.

Dave is a great friend of mine who himself has broken through in his own life to give us a book unencumbered with the stereotypical restrictive view of life.

This book is a tool to help illuminate you to the endless possiblities of your life.

Gerard Keehan
Senior Minister at Sunset Coast Christian Life Centre, Perth, W. Australia

This is one of the best books I have read on "no-limits" living.

Dave Gilpin has taken many of life's challenges and lessons learned and distilled them into a catalogue of wisdom.

Steve Penny
Senior Pastor of Kings Christian Church, Sunshine Coast, Australia

Dave's book is down to earth, faith-building and easy to read. Anyone who is willing to think outside the box should read it.

Paul Scanlon
Senior Minister of Abundant Life Centre, Bradford, England

David Gilpin's uncompromising approach to Christian living is optimised in his reassessment of some well-known sayings. He turns their limited and negative aspect into an easy, understandable strategy for destiny living. You could become a positive Christian by reading this book!

David E Carr
Senior Minister at Renewal Christian Centre, Solihull, England

This unique book will undoubtedly become a Christian classic and its contents provide every reader with a resource for growing bigger in their own faith and also for helping others to see beyond their present horizons.

Rev. John Partington
Senior Minister at Riverside Christian Centre, Exeter

Dave Gilpin is one of the best leaders I know. This book reveals not only the depth of Dave's leadership gifting, but also the degree to which God has blessed him with a creative and insightful mind.

Mike Breen
Team Rector at St Thomas' Church, Sheffield, England

ACKNOWLEDGEMENTS

As a minister, I sometimes feel a little guilty that a lot of my thoughts actually originate from somebody else. My wife tells me that my preaching is so convincing that it doesn't matter, and that the people I nicked stuff from probably borrowed it from someone else anyway! (Special thanks to my soothing wife, Jenny!)

Here are some of those people to whom I am indebted, and whom I would like to thank: Brian Houston, Steve Penny, David Cartledge, Danny Guglielmucci, Wayne Alcorn, Paul Scanlon, and my favourite mentor – Charles Spurgeon (who's never going to complain about his stuff resurfacing after more than a century).

Thanks also to my mates Glyn and Sophia, and Colin and Dawn, and to my good friends Gerard and Sue.

INTRODUCTION

Ever since I was a young teenager living in Melbourne, Australia, I have followed the pop charts. It was the mid-seventies when both Elton John and David Soul ruled the airwaves. It is now the twenty-first century, and Elton John has both survived and conquered, while Mr Soul has been confined to the vaults of history. Save a remarkable comeback, the only remembrances of the man will come from shows entitled "Where are they now?" and re-runs of "Starsky and Hutch" (he was Hutch). My greatest prayer is to be saved from such a fate.

I don't want to be a "one-hit wonder". I don't want to be used by God for a short season and then left to reminisce about "the good old days".

As with the music industry, there are many factors that determine whether we have only one hit in life and at best become legends in our living room, or have hit after hit after hit and possibly become legends in the land. A lack of creativity would be a major factor. Courage and integrity

15

would also rate, as well as passion and wisdom. For the Christian, hearing and obeying the voice of God would be essential, as well as an increasing inner capacity to keep on keeping on.

All of these factors together define SQ – spiritual intelligence. It is a form of intelligence that works like an engine strategically employing every aspect of wisdom, knowledge, inspiration and application, resulting in the power to create hit after hit.

It is God's will that you go from glory to glory and from strength to strength. It is His will that you have ever-increasing spheres of influence for the Kingdom of God. Your world requires more than one magic answer and more than one word from God. It requires an intelligence that is more akin to that required for a game of chess than for snakes and ladders.

SQ looks at 21 strategies to increase your spiritual intelligence. Its launch pad is 21 of the world's most popular sayings. They say "Don't re-invent the wheel" and "Beggars can't be choosers". Spiritual intelligence begs to differ. They say "Don't count your chickens before they hatch" and "You can't have your cake and eat it too". Spiritual intelligence looks at making a bigger cake!

This book is not about positive thinking or about possibility-thinking. You can be positively negative about the possibility that all doors are closed! This book is not just about thinking differently; it is about an understanding and a synergy of elements that work together to keep you on the edge of your God-given endeavours.

Finally, this book is for everyone who wants their future to be greater than their past. It is for those who believe their "average" is enough of an enemy to merit being locked in history's vaults with Mr Soul. Here's to the hit-makers and the future.

David Gilpin

PS Why not try the SQ test at www.v3leadership.comsqtest to find out your current level of spiritual intelligence?

You can do this at three strategic times. Firstly, do it now, before you read the book, to see where you currently stand. Secondly, do it immediately after reading the book, and, thirdly, take the test twelve weeks after finishing in order to give yourself time to meditate on and assimilate the truths contained therein.

Enjoy boosting your spiritual intelligence!

It's the early bird
that catches the worm!

but it's the second mouse
that gets the cheese . . .

YOU CAN HAVE YOUR CAKE
AND EAT IT TOO

"Free line rental, you say."

They say, "you can't have your cake and eat it too". *I* say it's time to make a bigger cake! You can then both have it *and* eat it if you enlarge it. So often we're held back by the resources available to us and, instead of breaking into the realm of the supernatural, we remain earthbound. Some have found ways of being prudent with the cake that they've

Blessed are the cake makers!

been given and try to cut it up into smaller pieces to make it last as long as possible. I remember winning a competition in my late teens by cutting a chocolate wrapper into one continuous strand. I made a strand that was a metre long and shrugged off the competition. I made the most of what I had, and won! Our Christianity, however, is designed to take us out of the limitations of what we have, into the realm of what we don't have. It crosses the line that divides the natural from the supernatural.

Living on the edge

In the gospel of John there is a story about a disabled man who had lived by a pool for 38 years, unable to get better (John 5:1–9). It tells us that, at a certain time, when the water was supernaturally stirred, the first one into the water was the one who got healed. Jesus asked the man a question: "Do you want to be made well?" It was an excellent question. The man had obviously got used to his poolside surroundings. He had probably grown quite popular amongst the other people waiting for healing. He might have found unexpected status amongst the poor. He might have got a respectable income from begging or been comfortably supported by an uncle or a brother. He would have had a suntan to die for! Did he really want to be made well, was the pertinent question to ask.

Some people love to complain about their circumstances but do nothing about them. They are full of excuses as to why something cannot be done. The disabled man had two excuses. Firstly, he said no one was around to help him into the pool when the waters were stirred. Secondly, someone always beat him to the water. Why was he not living on the edge, ready to fall in at the slightest sign of rippled waters? He was not bedridden, he was excuse-ridden!

On February 11th 2001, Ellen Macarthur became the youngest person to sail single-handedly around the world. She was just 24 years of age. Despite her longest sleep being two hours and 48 minutes over a 94-day marathon, and striking a semi-submerged container, she made history. She beat off every excuse as to why she could not win, and won.

Around 70 years ago, Glen Cunningham had a dream of breaking the world record for the mile run. One day Glen and his brother went down to a one-room Kansas schoolhouse to start the morning fire. They poured kerosene on and an explosion caused their clothes to catch fire. His brother died and the doctor said that Glen would not live long. At the age of 18, he could not walk, yet he would have his father hitch up the horses to the walking plough, carry him out there and tie his hands to the handle because he could not hang on all day. He would lean against the crossbar as he was dragged around the wheat fields in an attempt to remobilise his legs. At the age of 22, Glen Cunningham still could not walk but he had learnt to move with both a crutch and a cane. At the age of 25, he broke the world record for the mile run. He would not be contained by his circumstances.

In 1660, John Bunyan was arrested for preaching without a licence. He was jailed for twelve years. Instead of sinking into an excuse-ridden world, he wrote one of the world's greatest stories, *Pilgrim's Progress*.

Containment or advancement

One of Satan's greatest aims is not to send you backwards. His aim is to prevent you from going forwards

One of Satan's greatest aims is not to send you backwards. His aim is to prevent you from going forwards. Containment is his aim. He wants to keep you living by the pond, not swimming in the ocean. Did you know that things grow according to the size of the environment they live in? The size of both a shark and a goldfish is determined by the size of the pond in which they live. A shark can triple in size by being released from its container. An adult elephant that was restrained as an infant by a three-metre chain will continue to live within a radius of three metres, even after the chain is removed. It is essential that we plant ourselves in an environment that expands our horizons and encourages growth.

I once met a minister called Phil Baker[1] from Perth in Australia. I asked him what new things he was doing in his church and he said that he had hired the Western Australian Symphony Orchestra. "I didn't think you could do that," I replied in amazement, and enquired whether they played Beethoven's Ninth or the 1812 Overture. He told me they played Hillsong Music! He used them for an outreach and had paid a company to write the score. The results were that many got saved and were added to the church. He had made a bigger cake!

Visitation or inhabitation?

The second thing that held back the man by the pool at Bethesda was that he was looking for an angelic visitation. He was looking for a special moment, even while Jesus stood beside him. Many people spend their whole lives looking for a visitation from God. I remember watching a reporter interview Maurice Green, the Olympic gold medal holder and the fastest man to run the one hundred metres. It was just before his one-hundred-metre race at a European track event where it was slightly wet and the wind conditions were not perfect. The reporter asked Maurice if that day would be a world-record day. He immediately retorted, "*Every* day is a world-record day." Every day was an opportunity for greatness. He was not boxed in by circumstance or waiting for a special moment.

Roger Bannister was told that it was scientifically impossible for a man to run a mile in less than four minutes. In 1954 he became the first man to do so. In the following year, 37 other men followed him and, within two years, over 300 had broken the four-minute mile.[2] In 1999 the record stood at three minutes 43.13 seconds – around fifteen seconds faster than Bannister's own time. How's that for stepping out of containment? Solomon tells us in his book of Ecclesiastes that "whoever watches the wind will not plant; whoever looks at the clouds will not reap" (Eccles. 11:4). He goes on to say, "As you do not know the path of the wind or how the body is formed in a mother's womb, so you cannot understand the work of God, the Maker of all things. Sow your seed in the morning, and at evening let not your hands be idle, for you do not know which will succeed, whether this or that, or whether both will do equally well" (Ecclesiastes 11:5–6). You need to stop waiting for the right time and start to sow into a bigger future. Right time, right now.

You need to stop waiting for the right time and start to sow into a bigger future

There are many Christians who are waiting for a special visitation that is not coming. The foundation of New Testament Christianity is that the Holy Sprit has come to inhabit, not just to visit. The greatest strength a saint has is the knowledge that God will *not* be visiting them. Why? Because he never left! He lives with us. When we wake up in the morning, no matter how we feel, the same power that raised Christ from the dead dwells within us. The same power that is moving across Africa through the ministry of Reinhardt Bonnke dwells within us. The same power that lived and worked through Paul lives within us. We do not wake up to a distant God, we wake up to a God who has made His home in us. *You* did not find God. *He* found *you*. *You* do not have to chase Him to be blessed. *He* pursues you. *He* wants to give you a hope and a future. Every day is filled with divine opportunity, regardless of whether you feel it or not. God's word declares that we are blessed in the heavenly realms with every spiritual blessing in Christ. It has already been accomplished. It has already been done. See beyond your limitations! Open your eyes to the possibilities all around you. Zaccheus' are in the trees, and it is time for us to look up and take notice. Even though we all want more of God's presence, the truth is that it was with us all along – we were simply unaware of it. Jacob was so caught up with the hatred of his brother and the uncertainty of his future that he thought the place he slept in was far from God. After a God-given dream and a God-given promise, he awoke and said, "Surely the Lord is in this place, and I was not aware of it" (Gen. 28:16). Rise in confidence, for God is with you. Look for God-given opportunities in your life, starting with today. Don't look for pie in the sky; make a cake that is big enough both to eat and to have at the same time.

Pay it forward

The disabled man was preoccupied with waiting to be set free. Jesus said to him, "Rise, take up your bed, and walk" (John 5:8). Each of these three actions is forward-facing. In fact, the whole of the Bible is forward-facing. It is not focused on deliverance as much as it is on inheritance. The cross is not the destination for us, but a place at which we must die, receive forgiveness and move through to the resurrection. The children of Israel were in bondage in Egypt, but they were then set free. God promised them a land flowing with milk and honey. Their destiny was not to be one mile outside Egypt but right in the heart of Canaan. Many have made the Bible repentance-centred and not destiny-centred. Repentance leads us only to the doorway of our God-given future. We then need to step through it. The cross gave us the entry permit into our God-given future. Faith takes the permit and applies the promises. Deliverance is only a means to an inheritance.

Deliverance is only a means to an inheritance

When Jesus said "Get up", he was declaring "Don't just lie there!" It is time to believe again. When he said "Pick up your bed", he was saying "You'll never be returning to this place again". When he said "Walk" it was both a walk away from the life the man had been living and a walk into a brand-new life. A lot of people hang around the place of failure after being healed by God. They may be whole, but they remain weak, and inactive.

Most healing comes not from the prayer line, but from the pursuit of destiny. Many times I have felt the release of God when I've been on the way to future destiny. It is time to walk in the light, and take the sunshine-rays of revelation and apply them to our lives today (I John 1:5–7). It is time to walk in the Spirit, put on the regenerate man and leave our weak, sin-bound self at the cross (Galatians 5:6). It is time to walk in newness of life and take hold of the largeness of our destiny in Christ (Romans 6:4).

We all live under the same sky, but we don't all have the same horizon

Someone once said that "we all live under the same sky, but we don't all have the same horizon".[3] The time has come to expand your horizons. You can both have your cake and eat it too. Either bake a bigger cake, or bake two for good measure!

YOU CAN BOTH LEAD A HORSE TO WATER AND MAKE IT DRINK

"Oi!"

They say that you can lead a horse to water, but you can't make it drink. Wrong! You just need a thirsty horse. A horse that is thirsty will break fences to quench its craving. Thirst is a powerful driving force that pushes people on to do the extreme. Leadership, whether it be leading a home, a business or a church, is all about creating a thirst in people's mouths. Self-motivation is a powerful energy which, when harnessed, produces incredible results. I am amazed at all the energy that is expended in trying to get people to do things that they don't want to do. The reward is despondency and disillusionment in the leader and the follower. The best way to get anyone to do anything isn't to demand it, but to get them to see it and want it.

29

Vision creates thirst

Vision creates a thirst and a hunger to have what is invisible. It creates an attainable dream that both excites and motivates. No one can motivate themselves. Motivation is a by-product of hope. You cannot just "get motivated". It is the vision – the dream – the hope of realisation, that creates the motivation. If I said to someone that I wanted them to go to an athletics track to train for six hours daily, they would certainly ask why. If I said I wanted them to train every day, including Christmas Day, not once, but twice, they would flatly refuse. But if I told them that if they did it they were guaranteed to become the greatest, most successful Olympian that Britain had ever produced, they might perhaps think again.

This is what Daley Thompson did to become the world's most successful all-round athlete. In 1976, at 17 years of age, he got a taste of the Olympic spirit. He came eighteenth. That taste and the thirst for gold led him to follow a legendary training programme that was more extreme than that of any other athlete in his class. It paid off. He won his first gold in 1980 and his second in Los Angeles in 1984. If it had not been for injury, he would have won his third gold in 1988, coming as it was only 150 points from winning.[1]

Commitment is the child of vision

Someone once said that "commitment is the child of vision".[2] Most people are not led by vision, but by a sense of duty. When that happens, life falls to its lowest common denominator. It becomes boring and monotonous. People start suffering from ME – minimum effort. Times with God become a drudge when we're only there "to do time". I remember spending 60 minutes with God every day over many months. After a while it became an effort to do the full duration and became a source of condemnation when I could only pull off 55 minutes. Eventually I quit. When I first got saved, I carried around with me a piece of paper on which I wrote down all the things I needed to correct about who I was and what I did. The list was huge. It came from a

> *Most people are not led by vision, but by a sense of duty*

personality that was prone to perfectionism. I found that I had some excellent days and some really bad days. What I felt I needed was to be more committed. In fact, most of the sermons I heard were on commitment. I always felt that a lack of commitment was my problem. Fortunately, I have now changed my whole approach to life. I am more committed than ever, and I am not driven by self-analysis. I rarely suffer from condemnation and I now know that, most of the time, God is really pleased with me. I have become vision-led. The vision I hold close is God's vision of me. I am chosen, called, adopted, forgiven, raised up and anointed with the Holy Spirit. I am blessed, accepted, alive, and destined for greatness. In fact, God hand-selected me before I was born. Such is the destiny upon my life! It is also the destiny upon your life.

The trophy room

A few years back I remember seeing the look on British Athletics star Jonathan Edwards' face when he stood on the rostrum at the World Athletics Championship. He had come third and disappointment was written all over him. He knew that he could have done far better. It was a bitter blow. He went home to England defeated, but he didn't stay defeated. I suspect that not long after his return home he went into his trophy room and saw all the medals he'd won for his special greatness at the triple jump. Before long, his head would have risen, his shoulders lifted and his spirit revived as he saw the name written on every medal: Jonathan Edwards. He was that man! He returned to training and, within a short time, he had won the most coveted medal in the world – the gold at the Sydney Olympics. The book of Ephesians begins with the trophy room – your trophy room. In that room is a gold medal with the inscription "chosen by God". In the corner there is a medallion with the word "adopted" etched into it. In the showcase, sparkling like crystal, is a vase with the words "highly favoured" written on it. All around are medals of honour and on each is etched your name.

In the corner there is a medallion with the word "adopted" etched into it

Ephesians chapters one, two and three are about you! It is God's vision for you. It gives God great pleasure to present you with your own trophy room. Christ leads by vision. If a team is doing badly at half time, a worthy manager will tell them they have the ability and capacity to win. He will go back through past achievements and successes and then say that winning is attainable. With added strategy and a good kick from behind, the manager has done the best that he can. That's how God leads His team. When we come to Him, He reminds us of all that Christ has won for us. He walks us slowly through the trophy room. Our heads begin to lift and our shoulders begin to rise in the presence of the greatest leader of all time.

When vision returns we are then ready for the corrections and the discipline that will help us achieve our goals.

Ephesians chapter 4 verse 1 is the pivotal hinge between vision and its child, called commitment. Paul writes, "As a prisoner for the Lord, then, I urge you to live a life worthy of the calling you have received." It is time to match our call with our behaviour. The book of Ephesians goes on to deal with the pulling up of our socks!

An audience of one

If you want to do well in life, always begin with vision. I remember sitting in McDonald's a few years ago and I felt that God was encouraging me that He was my greatest fan. For a number of months I visited McDonald's every morning both to enjoy an Egg McMuffin and a coffee and to meditate on the word of God. Every day, the tears would flow as I pondered His encouragement of me. The big pop groups can have thousands of fans who buy their CDs and wear their T-shirts, but I've realised there's nothing quite like having an audience of one when it is God himself.

When my wife used to get out on the running track as a teenager, she used to look for her dad in the grandstand. Her dad was a sales representative but he always tried to make it to her track events on special occasions. Jenny's father was bald, and this helped her locate his whereabouts in the stands. Whenever Jenny saw him, she ran faster. She was running for her dad, and he was cheering her on. That's what God is doing for you right now – cheering you on. The Bible says that "if God is for us, who can be against us?" (Romans 8:31). It also says "Who shall separate us from the love of Christ?" (Romans 8:35). God's love "always protects, always trusts, always hopes, always perseveres" (1 Corinthians 13:7). He is your greatest fan. He believes in you. He chose you before the foundation of the earth. You were a success *before* you were born! In you is all the potential and workmanship of God.

---

*He is your
greatest fan*

Take a trip today through your personal trophy room and then start to walk a walk that says "snap" to the incredible calling to which you were called.

LET YOUR EYES BE BIGGER
THAN YOUR STOMACH

"Michaelangelo! How many times have I warned you about painting on the walls?"

They say, "Your eyes are bigger than your stomach." They *ought* to be! Your ability to see your future should be greater than your ability to accomplish it. My boy loves buffets. He gets excited when he knows there is one approaching, and, since the church I pastor believes in hospitality, there's always one for him to look forward to. With bulging eyes, he attempts to pile as much as he can onto his plate and then tries to eat it. From his point of view, the problem is not that his eyes are bigger than his stomach but that his stomach is too small for his eyes. The wisdom of only putting on your plate what you can comfortably digest is good for the body, but no good for breaking into divine possibilities. Your eyes don't need to get smaller; your stomach just needs to get bigger!

Seeing is believing

People cut life according to the cloth available and not according to their God-given vision. Your life in God is determined not by the size of your talent or wallet, but by your ability to see as God sees. A craftsman and a hobbyist are very different in the way they go about things. A hobbyist gathers all the bits he can find and, after looking them over, says to himself, "I'll see what I can make." A craftsman takes his dream and declares, "I'll make what I can see." Seeing really *is* believing.

One day two blind men pursued Jesus, crying out, "Son of David, have mercy on us." Jesus asked them if they believed He was able to heal them. Their reply was a definitive "Yes". Jesus touched their eyes and declared, "According to your faith will it be done to you." Their eyes were opened (Matthew 9:27–31).

Faith determined their outcome. Faith has eyes to see the future as God sees it. It has been remarked that "eyes that look are common, but eyes that see are rare!"[1]

When attempting to purchase a building that would house the vision of our growing church, I had several interesting meetings with the owner. The building was

Eyes that look are common, but eyes that see are rare!

formerly owned by Spear and Jackson and was once the factory that made their legendary garden tools. Sheffield, known as the steel city, once met 50% of Europe's stainless steel demand and this building, near the city centre, is a memento of a bygone era. With little in the bank, the owner suggested that we buy or lease one of the three floors available. It was an attractive offer, and after a couple of weeks had passed I began to think that he might be right. Shortly after this my receptionist came to me with a strong word of advice taken from a Bible story about a young woman called Ruth. One day, her mother-in-law, Naomi, sensing the destiny between Ruth and a man called Boaz, encouraged Ruth to make a bold move toward Boaz by sleeping at his feet one night. Although I certainly did not feel I wanted to sleep at the feet of the owner of this building, I got the message!

Ruth wanted Boaz's hand in marriage. I really wanted all three storeys of this building. God spoke to me: "Don't downsize your vision in times of difficulty." To cut a long story short, we bought *all* three storeys in a sensational deal and now it is one of the largest church buildings in the whole of Great Britain. According to your faith be it unto you.

The most important thing to know about faith is that it is the currency of heaven. If I went to Australia and bought a car, I would pay in dollars. If I went to France, I would pay in euros. You can't use one country's currency to pay for another country's goods. Likewise, Paul's letter to the Romans expressly says that we access the grace of God by faith (Romans 5:2). Faith is the currency of heaven – not sacrifice or works, but faith. Faith accesses grace. Our works of service are a necessary transport of our faith to the Bank of Grace, but the transaction is in response to our faith. God's grace is His divine, undeserved favour towards us. It is more than justification and forgiveness. It includes peace, joy and power as well as all His provision for the vision. Your faith is a precious commodity. Build a hothouse environment about you and protect your God-given gift.

Believe it or not!

Faith comes from hearing from God (Romans 10:17). You can't make it up. It is a divine original, a unique revelation, a special word to you from God. You can't say to someone, "Get some faith". Faith is a by-product of listening to the voice of God. If you've heard from God, you've got faith. It is not an emotion. It is a deep-rooted conviction that God will do what He said He'd do. Eventually, this conviction at the core of your being needs to infiltrate your mind and should be evidenced by various faith actions.

The devil's great trick is to make you believe that you had faith on Sunday but that it has gone by Monday. Not true. If you really had it on Sunday, you've still got it on Monday. Don't believe the enemy's lies! In fact, many Christians have thousands of seeds of faith already planted in their spirit from those times when God has spoken to them. They may seem to be non-existent, but don't believe it. If you continue to think and live according to your faith, you will then see God-given harvests – according to your faith.

The Tarrant spirit

I often tell people to be aware of the "Tarrant spirit". Chris Tarrant is the highly successful anchorman of the great British re-invention of the game show *Who Wants to be a Millionaire?* The contestant might be certain the answer is Napoleon, and declares their intention of running with that answer. But, after a pregnant pause, Chris Tarrant leans over and says, "Confident?" His job is simply to sow a seed of doubt. The contestant now reviews their answer, and questions their convictions. It could be Alexander the Great, but they stick with Napoleon. After another long pause Chris Tarrant says, "Sure?" That sends the contestant into a flurry of indecision. It is these long delays of doubt that are edited from the show so that it is viewer-friendly. The answer could now be Ivan the Terrible, Genghis Khan, Napoleon or Alexander the Great. Finally, the contestant begins to swell with the rising confidence that they started with and boldly declares what they knew all along. In response to further interrogation, they now add the words, "Without a shadow of a doubt," and accordingly, Napoleon is lit up irreversibly in green on the screen. They are then told that they had £32,000 and now they have (long pause) £64,000. Chris takes his opportunity for a quick game-show hug.

The Tarrant spirit almost won. It is designed to cast over the contestant a shadow of doubt. It is so important, after hearing from God, to stay away from shadows. Doubt is the enemy of faith. Doubt actually means "to stand in two ways" or a "wavering between two opinions". The shadow of doubt is an oscillation between the word of God being true, and the word of God being false. Make a decision today to stand on what God says and refuse to come under the shadow of doubt. Jesus said that if you have faith and don't doubt then you can see even the mountains move! (Mark 11:22–24)

Can you have more faith?

Often people say that it takes more faith to believe for a million pounds than it does to trust for ten pounds. Not necessarily! To a Bible college student, ten pounds can be like a million! What you need today will take faith. What you need in ten years will take faith. It is simply faith for different things.

Reinhardt Bonnke does not necessarily have more faith than you do in his mission to see Africa saved. Did God speak to you about Africa? Probably not. God spoke to Reinhardt, and faith resulted. Hopefully, you are in the place that God has spoken to *you* about. You've got faith. Reinhardt has faith. This example shows that we don't have less faith, just faith for different things! Stop comparing yourself with others. You have a unique call and a great measure of faith. You can only be a better *you*, not a better someone else. Life is not always about having *more* faith, but having less doubt – closing down the deceptive voice that tells you that you can't, and sticking with your real convictions.

> *You can only be a better you, not a better someone else*

It is time to enlarge your eyes. It is time to see the future as God sees it and let your capacity, your spiritual stomach, catch up with your vision. Within you already are seeds of faith that are destined to bring about an incredible harvest. Value those seeds as incredibly precious and protect them with all you've got.

REINVENT THE WHEEL

"Aw, leave 'em – they'll be bored with it by tomorrow."

They say, "Let's not reinvent the wheel." Everything needs a good reinvention! If the wheel had not been reinvented on a regular basis, then we would still be riding on wheels of stone, like Fred Flintstone. Rubber tyres were introduced in the mid-1800s. Thank God for Mr Goodyear! Every wheel design has its advantages and disadvantages. Stone wheels were very good, but too brittle and too heavy. Spoked wheels were good, but too weak for heavyweights, and even pneumatic tyres get punctures. Right now, there's a tyre revolution going on. Solid tyres are gradually replacing bicycle tyres around the world, with the same bounce-factor as an inflatable tyre. No more punctures, and no more pumping!

Become a master of reinvention

We need to become masters of reinvention. They say, "If it ain't broke, don't fix it." That kind of thinking is unproductive. James Dyson invented a new-style vacuum cleaner in Great Britain that was rejected by both Hoover and General Electric. With over 100 patents, including a new bagless system with no loss of suction, Dyson was forced to start his very own production company. Today, across Britain, "Dysons" are the fastest-selling vacuum appliances. He reinvented the Hoover! Most pop bands are either one-hit-wonders or live according to their predictable three-year sell-by date. They fail to reinvent. Madonna, however, has mastered this principle of reinvention. Despite the fact that she has been making popular music since the 1980s, she still produced a best-selling album in 2001, and her sell-out Earl's Court show in London was the buzz of the media for weeks. Struggling along, every older artist that teams up with a new up-and-comer is attempting reinvention.

Many people only experience one move of God in their lives – they surf one wave and then fail to make the adjustment to ride the next wave

Likewise, many people only experience one move of God in their lives – they surf one wave and then fail to make the adjustment to ride the next wave. They fail to reinvent.

The biblical word for reinvent is "transform". It declares that, as we get a clear and fresh vision of Jesus, we are transformed into that vision and go from one stage of glory to the next (2 Corinthians 3:18). It says that as we allow our minds to be transformed we can then experience, in full measure, God's will for our lives (Romans 12:2). This word comes from the Greek word from which we get the English word, "metamorphic". A metamorphic rock, such as granite, bears no resemblance to the molten lava that poured out of the volcano thousands of years before, yet that is where it comes from. The caterpillar who saw a butterfly said to his friend, "You'll never catch me going up in one of those." "One of those" is actually one of *him*, after a transformation – after metamorphosis. It is a vital part of our life experience. People often say to me that I have changed, I'm different. They say it in a complimentary way and often it is within the context of my preaching ministry. I like that. In fact, there would be something wrong if that were not the case. I want to stagger people who have not seen me in years. In fact, I want to be barely recognisable! I want to be transformed from glory to glory.

Reinvention inventory

There are five things about you that Christ wants regularly to reinvent.

Your heart

Firstly we need a "change of heart". Proverbs calls the heart the wellspring of life (Proverbs 4:23). Out of your heart flow the boundaries of your life. Jesus said the good man brings good things out of the good stored up in him, and the evil man brings evil things out of the evil stored up in him (Matthew 12:35). God's aim is to give you a heart that is just like His. He wants a soft heart, a generous heart and a pure heart because He is aware that out of it flow the events of life. Because a spring is the outcome of a supply in the heart of the earth, we can truthfully say that tomorrow's world will be determined by today's heart. If you allow your heart to be expanded, you can be assured. In the Old Testament we find a man called Jabez. He was named Jabez because, when his mother gave birth to him, she gave birth in pain. His name means pain. He caused others pain and life caused *him* great pain. He decided to cry out to God for him to enlarge his territory and keep him from harm and pain. God granted his request and broke him free from the "nature" or "name" that had determined his world (1 Chronicles 4:10).

When someone asks you how things are going, make sure you answer with how your heart is going, not your harvest. Heart determines harvest. If you want a large harvest, ask God to give you a larger heart.

God wants to create a reinvented heart in us to use adversity to produce advancement. Adversity does not create character; it only reveals it. It is our decisions that create the change. Find out where you are frustrated in your life, and there you'll find God's construction site for a new and reinvented heart. When you have done your best and it is not good enough, God is developing a heart of trust. When you have lost money on a project and God challenges you to give away what is left, He is developing a heart of faith. When you are on the cross for something that you never did and never said, God is developing a heart of love. The challenge then is to bless your enemy. Resurrections come from funerals and reinventions come when the old has had its day. Be smart and follow the cry of David, "Create in me a pure heart, O God, and renew a steadfast spirit within me" (Psalm 51:10).

Adversity does not create character, it only reveals it. It is our decisions that create the change

Your personality

Secondly, He wants to reinvent your personality. "Well that's just the way I am" or "that's just who you married" are the words of one-hit wonders: people who fail to reinvent. It is often not true. People who are shy and introverted when they are 38 were nothing of the sort when they were eight. What happened through their teen years and into their twenties that changed them? God wants to change your personality and make it into the personality that you were born to be.

I have always been overly sensitive. Because I have a melancholic side to my personality, I would often internalise stuff to the point of obsession. I would replay what others said time and time again and feel myself being sucked down the plughole. One of the methods that God has used to change me has been to place me into situations that were too big for me to handle. He would put me with people who had the ability to make me feel small. He would put me into situations where, without the right decisions, I would be crushed by people's opinions. Instead of downsizing life according to my former personality, God upsized my life and changed my personality through helping me in the decisions I made during the challenging times. Instead of being intimidated by people, I chose to be inspired. Instead of being crushed by people's opinions, I chose to rise above them and listen to the opinions of God. I have developed a God-confidence and a godly audacity that have come by revelation and by making the right decisions in the midst of great challenges. The quicksand that was in my life, to which so many melancholics are susceptible, has hardened up. People say that I am always enthusiastic and positive. That is the outcome of the power of reinvention.

Your lifestyle

The third thing that God wants to reinvent is your lifestyle. It is the kerb that defines the road of your life. It should regularly change. Some people want to legalise the way you spend time with God. They say that when you are with God, you ought to do a number of things, such as pray for a certain length of time and regularly read through the Bible. I find that the way I relate to God varies on a seasonal basis. Sometimes I am simply a "master-asker" for the blessing of God; other months I am lost in worship and or I might be mostly meditative upon the word of God. We all love a good routine, but we need to be aware when the razor has lost its sharpness. Lifeless religion specialises in blunt razors.

Don't ever get discouraged in the transition time between two seasons. Between every gear change on the road of life, we go into neutral. Build a lifestyle that best expresses the emphasis of God at that time. If it is family, then build in family time. If it is strategy; then build in time away. A good, healthy lifestyle is rarely totally balanced. As we walk, we don't roll but we go from one foot to the next – our weight distribution changes! Do not let your lifestyle be a hindrance. Be disciplined enough to build a lifestyle that is focused, but be wise enough to know that it is only a vehicle to get you from A to B, not from A to C.

> *Lifeless religion specialises in blunt razors*

Your ministry

I used to say I was an evangelist because all I did was evangelise. I got bored with pastoring and hated team-time. "Just get me out there with the lost" was the cry of my heart. There are gifts in all of us that lie dormant like seeds in a bag. Timothy had to stir up the gift of God within him and not define himself by his current ministry success and limitations (2 Timothy 1). That's the problem of gift analysis: it can define you too closely. Some say "I'm just a helper" or "I'm a prophet", but the fact is, you've got a variety of gifts within you. God's gifts and ministries should be defined periodically within you. They emerge and submerge depending on season, usage and openness to reinvention. Others like to pigeonhole us for their own sense of security. Refuse it and allow God to make you all you were called to be.

Your appearance

The fifth thing to reinvent is your appearance and the appearance of the things around you. This is practically the only area the world deals with. Even though a concern with appearance can be prone to worldliness, we should never throw the baby out with the bath water. A change of appearance is either an illustrative end to a process of inward reinvention or a symbolised beginning of a complete overhaul. When I see someone who has been in hard times turn up with a new hairstyle or new clothes, I often celebrate. I deliberately say they look good, and it is so often true! I am not talking about being a slave to fashion or being driven by insecurity, but allowing the new appearance either to reflect an otherwise hidden process of change, or to define something new. To change an office around or change the bedroom around can work wonders in defining a new start.

To buy a new shirt when life has almost knocked you out can be prophetic. There was a season in my ministry when people were leaving church by the droves. Spurred on by a small minority, others lost confidence in my leadership. It looked like the wheels were falling off! People had started to notice an increased personal confidence that had come from a secret time of heart reinvention. No longer was I abdicating leadership decisions, I was now making them. This began to shake the security of those I had been leaning on for years. I no longer asked "What do you think?" ten times a day. I became more assertive. Assertiveness can easily be misread as arrogance rather than as evidence of a growing God-confidence. In the midst of it all, I had had a revelation that I was called by God and not by man. I was called by God and was the right man, in the right place, at the right time. Like the card game, I said "snap" to this fresh revelation and went down to a well-known department store and selected a fancy tie to wear the following Sunday. Numbers were down, but I was the sharpest-looking minister in the country on that day. It was both prophetic and affirmative – a new day would dawn and it would start with me. The following week, I revisited the store and bought another tie. That Sunday, I looked even sharper. My tie collection was almost completely reinvented! The change in my style of dress on Sunday mornings signified a great new season in God.

Recently I congratulated a middle-aged man for dressing well throughout a time of long unemployment. He never let himself hold a pity party, or dismiss his own ability and give up. His situation would not define his life. He took the promise of God to heart and decided to dress as if he were already living in a new realm of prosperity. What a great example of reinvention! His appearance was a prophetic statement of what was to come. Within a week this man had his new job.

In 1920, the Ford Motor Company was making one car every minute and the Model T accounted for around 60% of the entire market. The sales of General Motors stood at around twelve per cent, and they were hungry for a greater cut of the market. They developed the slogan "A car for every person and every purpose". They marketed five types of car: the Chevrolet, the Oldsmobile, the Pontiac, the Buick and the Cadillac. Each was updated on a regular basis and came in more than one colour. Henry Ford, when referring to the colour options offered for the Model T Ford, famously said, "Any colour – so long as it's black". By 1925, General Motors were outselling Ford. Ford failed to reinvent whilst General Motors developed a culture of reinvention.

Do not be left behind in the market place of life. Let us not be answering questions that no one is asking. Find yourself being reinvented for maximum effectiveness in today's world.

BEGGARS CAN BE CHOOSERS

"They want your mother's maiden name before they authorise the transaction, mate."

They say beggars can't be choosers. I beg to differ! Beggars get what they beg for. What you accept, you cannot change, and what you do not cry out for, you cannot have. Begging is a biblical concept. Accepting whatever comes along is not. Often we are too proud to beg. We associate begging with poverty and the bottom of the pile, but God is drawn to those who ask. If you beg with a big heart, a positive attitude and an expectant faith, you'll have a good chance of getting. Jesus' ministry speaks volumes to us about begging.

In Luke 11, God encourages us to become mega beggars and master askers. Jesus gives the story about the midnight munchies. A man had a visit from a friend at midnight and the pantry was bare. He went next door and woke up his

God encourages us to become mega beggars and master askers

neighbour for some bread. He kept knocking until he got a result! Jesus commented that it was not because of his relationship with his neighbour that the man got what he needed, but because of his "importunity". This is a strange word but it is translated as "persistence" in the New King James version of the Bible. Another translation uses the word "shamelessness". The man was audacious and tenacious. Jesus went on and said, "Ask and it will be given to you; seek and you will find; knock and the door will be opened to you. For everyone who asks receives; he who seeks finds; and to him who knocks, the door will be opened" (Luke 11:9–10). Audacity is something that we shun in western culture. Sometimes we use comments like "The audacity of the man!" when someone slips in ahead of us in a long queue. However, this is the spiritual attitude that Christ was extolling! It's cheeky, it's brazen and it's overstepping the mark. That mark or line in the sand has been drawn by a number of factors. Here are the top five:

We're conditioned not to ask

It begins at an early age. Often, if you opened your mouth at school and asked too many questions you would be open to ridicule – and that's just from the teacher. When we are young we are taught that it is rude for us to ask. It is interesting that the British are renowned for their ability to whinge. The problem is that they're taught to accept their situation and then inwardly moan about the consequences. If the food at the restaurant were too cold, an American would audaciously call for it to be removed and made right. American waiters are used to it and respond often with politeness and understanding. There is a demand to get it just right. The British would think it rude to complain and simply put up with the coldness of the meal. In fact, British waiters often get their knickers in a knot when challenged about the restaurant's standards. If the food has been taken away for a re-heat, who knows what's really been added to the food on return! Accepting the unacceptable produces frustration, and whinging is the outcome. What you accept, you cannot change. When Jacob grabbed hold of the angel at the ford of Jabbok, he said, "I won't let you go unless you bless me" (Genesis 32:26). He lost all dignity in his cry for help. Life changed dramatically for Jacob from that moment. His mega-begging and master-asking were the key to a mega breakthrough.

> *What you accept, you cannot change*

We quit too easily

We think that to ask once is the key to breakthrough, and if it doesn't happen it will never happen. God's favour, though, is poured out onto the hungry in heart. He is not keen on dainty, common, casual nibblers, but on desperate and hungry people! He loves desperation when it is directed towards Him. Desperation often leads to faith.

Whenever I'm driving somewhere with my son and we see anything that resembles a theme park, I am bombarded with the "can we, can we, can we?" mantra. Sometimes if I notice a giant slide, I'll draw attention to the other side of the road to escape a new auditory bombing campaign! The end result is that theme parks of whatever size are highly frequented. It is hard for dads to resist. If something fits my mission for him and my timetable of priorities, then I'll do it, but almost always in request to him asking. To ask, knock and seek is to persist until you get what you're looking for. God is goading us to try it out.

Persistence has been a key that has opened many doors of discovery. On 19th October 1879, Thomas Edison successfully demonstrated the electric light bulb after a two-year search for a filament and a design to keep the filament burning. Some say it took around six thousand attempts.[1] The bulb kept glowing for around 40 hours. Through sheer persistence and a little ingenuity, Edison patented one thousand and ninety-three inventions in his lifetime. He once said that "success is one per cent inspiration and ninety-nine per cent perspiration". Success is often getting up one more time than the one who failed. After six sessions of prayer and six visits by Elisha's servant to the top of the mountain, there were still no signs of the coming rains prophesied by Elijah to King Ahab. It was only on the seventh visit of his servant that a small cloud appeared, rising out of the sea (1 Kings 18:41–44). It was the start of a miracle that was longed for, but it took persistence to get it.

Success is often getting up one more time than the one who failed

We think that whatever will be, will be

Many think that, whether we pray or don't pray, everything is on a calendar that is predetermined by God. *The Truman Show* is one of the great movies of our time, in which Jim Carrey plays a man called Truman who is born into a world that is actually a huge set created by a television production company. His wife has been arranged; his job pre-determined and the events of each day planned to a tee. The movie charts his realisation that something is wrong and his subsequent attempts to break out, which he eventually succeeds in doing. People think life is like the Truman Show. They mistake everything that happens for the will of God, as if they were simply puppets on a stage.

The truth is that God created man to be in partnership with him. He is so committed to this partnership that He has decided to work *through* us not despite us or beside us. When it comes to evangelism, Paul writes, "We are therefore Christ's ambassadors, as though God were making His appeal through us. We implore you on Christ's behalf: Be reconciled to God" (2 Corinthians 5:20). So often we pray for God to do it, and He will – as long as we are prepared to be the answers to our own prayers. He never asked us to pray for the harvest, but to pray for labourers for the harvest. That is true partnership.

James tells us, "You do not have, because you do not ask God" (James 4:2). If you want someone to be saved, pray for God to send labourers: ask Him! God is drawn to a desperate heart. God's perfect will is not inevitable: it comes from your partnership with Him in all that He wants to do.

We create our own censorship board

We intrinsically feel that our motives are wrong unless we are praying for the starving people of Africa. Anything to do with *us* and we doubt the purity of our intentions. If it is money we want, we think it is selfish. If it is a big church, it must be for the stroking of the ego. If it is for others, we think it is self-righteous. James is correct, in some circumstances, when he says you ask and do not receive, "because you ask with wrong motives, that you may spend what you get on your pleasures" (James 4:3). He is directing his words to the worldly and the carnal. It is important to ask God to purify your heart and it is important to crucify the flesh or "the old man" who is corrupt in all his ways. But, there is a new man in you, created in the image of God, and it is righteous for that new man to ask God to bless him. It is right for a son to look to his dad not only for his needs but also for his pleasures. Not everything that my son asks for is granted, but the discretion comes from *me* and not from him. Don't get too hung up on questioning the validity of your prayers; let God decide what is best for you. He wants to prosper us. He wants to bless us and He wants us to acknowledge fully that He is our source. God wants everyone to live a life of abundance. It is so important for us constantly to echo the words, "Praise Him from whom *all* blessings flow." He is our source. Open the floodgates of heaven over your life with a fresh release of mega-begging and master-asking.

We don't believe anyone is listening

We think that no answer means no one's home. Nothing could be further from the truth. The Bible says, "This is the confidence we have in approaching God, that if we ask anything according to His will, He hears us. And if we know He hears us – whenever we ask – we know that we have what we asked of Him" (1 John 5:14–15). Our confidence is not in answered prayer but in the fact that God hears us. So many people say after experiencing God answering their prayers that now they are confident He will do it again. If confidence comes from answers, then what were you like before God answered? The Bible clearly says that our confidence should lie in the fact that God hears us. Our confidence should not be in our ability to pray – our words are only words. If He hears us then it is as good as in the bag.

Our confidence is not in answered prayer but in the fact that God hears us

The five rules of mega-begging

There are five conditions or rules to becoming mega beggars, or master askers:

Ask according to His will

How do you know His will? Ask! The psalmist makes a great request: "Show me your ways, O Lord, teach me your paths; guide me in your truth and teach me . . ." (Psalm 25:4–5). His will is always His word and His will is always in line with who Jesus is and what Jesus does. Jesus said, "You may ask me for anything in my name, and I will do it" (John 14:14). "In my name" is actually expanded in the Amplified Bible to mean "in line with who I am and what I am doing".

Ask frequently

Be unreasonably persistent, like a dog with a bone. Remember that the word "ask" carries the idea of continually asking!

Ask abundantly

Jesus said "If you ask for *anything* in my name." "Anything" is a big kind of word. Obstacles, circumstances or even the laws of nature that God himself put in place do not limit it.

Ask obediently

The Bible says, "Dear friends, if our hearts do not condemn us, we have confidence before God and receive from Him anything we ask, because we obey His commands and do what pleases Him" (1 John 3:21–22). It is important that we are full of faith and also full of love towards each other. Unforgiveness can so easily lead to bitterness as well as cutting off our vital union with the Father.

Ask whatever you desire

It is time to get confident! I call this the master class of master asking. Jesus tells us, "If you remain in me and my words remain in you, ask whatever you wish, and it will be given you" (John 15:7). Simply put, "If you make God your house and not your hotel or hostel and make His word live and breathe in you, then your desires count. Tell God about them and He will do it". It is an amazing verse with amazing consequences. This is the time for you to get confident about your own walk with God and stop living on handouts. Start to claim the desires of your heart.

Beggars *can* be choosers. Low confidence and a slavish mentality can rob you of the great benefits of sonship in God's house. Stop accepting the lowest and reach for the highest. God is still able to do far more than any of us can imagine. Paradoxical as it may seem, it is time to expect the unexpected! A poverty mentality has no place in the kingdom of God. We are adopted into a great family and have been granted an awesome inheritance. It is time to beg "big-time" and choose the destiny that God has planned for us.

SQ #6
START TEACHING GRANNY
TO SUCK EGGS

"Come on, dearie. You teach me your new way to suck eggs and I'll show you how to make a wolfskin coat."

They say, "Don't teach your granny to suck eggs." Why not? Granny may be well versed in her familiar egg-sucking tradition, but does she own the patent on egg sucking? Surely not! There might be a better way to suck eggs! Just as there is more than one way to skin a cat, so there is more than one way to suck eggs. A granny's ability to see this will usually depend on how long Granny has been doing it her own special way.

Within all of us is a difficult granny! A difficult granny is just another name for the "RTC factor" – the Resistance To Change factor. It is part of our human nature and regularly needs crucifying. "This is the way we've always done it" is a sure sign that the RTC factor is alive and well.

59

I love it when people invent new ways of doing things. An Englishman called Thomas Newcomen invented the steam engine in the early 1700s. It was improved by James Watt later that century but it wasn't until the early 1800s, with the emergence of George Stevenson and his steam locomotive, that the real opposition began to rise up. Until then canal owners had had a corner on the transportation market. This new invention was in direct competition. Despite opposition from canal owners and farmers, Stevenson won approval to build and run both a freight and a passenger railway service between Liverpool and Manchester in 1830. "Stevenson's Rocket" was immortalised. The owners of the old idea resisted just about every new idea. Stevenson broke the "granny factor" not only in his own life, but also in the lives of others.

In 1964, Philip Knight got together with Bill Bowerman, his athletics coach, to form a company that would import Japanese running shoes in order to undercut the market leader, Adidas. In search of a better sale, Bowerman poured liquid rubber into his wife's waffle iron and then cut it and stuck it to the sole of a running shoe. In that same year of 1971, the swoosh logo was purchased for $35 from a university design student and Nike was born.[1] In the following year, four of the top marathon runners were wearing the "waffle soles". By the late 1990s they had captured almost half of the sports shoe market and made it into the top three most familiar brand names on the planet.

The British navy has lost more of its men to disease than through fighting on the high seas. Scurvy was the biggest killer. In 1740, a British admiral lost 1,400 out of 1,900 men, largely owing to the disease. The cure had been recognised as early as 1593, on a voyage by the British naval hero Richard

Hawkins. Despite all of this the admiralty did not order the taking of fruit juice on board until the end of the eighteenth century. Their drink typically became lime juice mixed with rum – hence the expression "limeys" for British sailors.

The spirit of the entrepreneur

The spirit of the entrepreneur is the true spirit of the church. An entrepreneur is always looking for new ways and opportunities to expand God's kingdom on earth. When God saw that the earth that He created was very dark, He said, "Let there be light." When He saw all was very wet, He created dry land. When He saw that it was barren, He created vegetation. He saw the gap and filled it. That is the spirit of the entrepreneur. So many people complain and fail to become proactive and solution-conscious. Some people can easily find the 99 reasons why something cannot be done. I like it when someone finds the one reason why it can be done, and attempts it. I love it when someone simply attempts it, then discovers the reason why it worked! The highly successful Doc Marten boot company owes its millions to a German army doctor called Klaus Maertens. After a skiing accident whilst taking time out from the front line, Klaus designed a boot that would protect his ankle from further damage. Instead of making excuses for his disability, he made history.

The spirit of the entrepreneur is the true spirit of the church

American Express was born from a demand for a more convenient way to shop. McDonald's was born out of a demand to have food in a hurry. In 1948, Dick and Maurice McDonald opened their first takeaway restaurant where customers could drive in and place their order in the first window and, within a minute, collect it at the next window. IKEA, noting the demand for flat-pack, self-assembly furniture, started from a tiny mail-order business. It has become a furniture giant.

With the spirit of the entrepreneur, David Livingstone left his mission station and headed to the densely populated area of North Africa. He was prompted to go by his friend Robert Moffet, who wrote to Livingstone and said, "I have seen the smoke of a thousand villages. There, no missionary has ever been. There, sir, is your field." When so many walked the well-worn path, Livingstone paved a new path to an unreached people and made history.[2] The church needs more Livingstones – people prepared to move out of their comfort zones and dare to attempt great things for God. The market-place of the souls of the masses awaits.

Teaching granny

I remember standing outside a 55,000-square-foot, three-storey building that was later to become the Mega Centre – the centre of operations for our church. I stood with another minister, who simply could not fathom the enormity of the building. With no encouragement and a look of disbelief he walked off, failing to catch the sense of adventure. For a period of time, we parted company. Trying to teach grannies can be a soul-destroying exercise. I have learned to teach only the teachable and argue with the open. For years, teachers and ministers have tried to convince people who simply are not listening. In John chapter 10, Jesus says the reason why the sheep follow the shepherd is that they know His voice.

Ministry is based on relationship and respect. Not everyone who comes to my church is one of my sheep. It wouldn't be right to tell them what to do; it would simply fall on deaf ears. I have a responsibility only to the sheep. Proverbs tells us that if we correct a mocker he will hate us all the more. We often make things worse for ourselves: we spend a lot of time trying to teach the unteachable and not enough time with the sheep of our pasture. It is often the squeaky wheel that gets the most attention. If it continues to squeak after it has been well oiled then there is a more serious problem.

> *Not everyone who comes to my church is one of my sheep*

Early adapters

The proof of a shepherd–sheep relationship is often the response time of the sheep. Whenever a new God-given direction is given, people fall into a number of categories. The early adapters are those who hear the word and put it into practice – some gladly, some not so gladly. The middle adapters check it out with the opinions of others and do serious battle with the RTC (Resistance to Change) factor. The late adapters are the ones who follow because everyone else has. The sheep of your pasture are more likely to be found in the first category than in the last. Early adaptation and discipleship go hand in hand. In Luke chapter 9, Jesus asked three people to follow Him and each gave an excuse as to why they wouldn't be following that day. He said to one, "Let the dead bury their own dead, but you go and proclaim the kingdom of God" (Luke 9:60). He realised the man was full of excuses. Discipleship is about being a "quick response unit" that is ready and available to carry out the shepherd's instructions. The leader's responsibility is to lead with vision and divinely inspired strategy, but it is the follower's role to come under that leadership.

In my church I am totally committed to the maxim "only do it if you want to do it". If you *have* to do it then the motive becomes blurred. I remember a time when I forgot a promised dinner date with my wife – I had made other arrangements. After realising the seriousness of my predicament, I said that it would be a "sacrifice", but I would do it. She responded curtly, "Well, if it's going to be such a sacrifice then you can have your dinner date alone. I'm not coming." A cold wind began to blow through the house! My wife only wanted the meal if *I* wanted it. Doing things out of a sense of duty is the lowest form of service. She wanted the best form of service that came from my willingness and desire to be a part of a great night.

It is time to break free of the granny within us and start to explore the possibilities that lie ahead of us through entertaining new ways of doing things. Take hold of the entrepreneurial spirit, and start to become teachable and pliable for the new things that God is saying.

START COUNTING YOUR CHICKENS BEFORE THEY HATCH

"Hey, Toni! 6 Tikka Masalas, 2 Kievs, 3 Sesame Buns and the veggie on Table 12 wants an omlette."

They say, "Don't count your chickens before they hatch." I say, "Start counting today!" Don't ever plan for disappointment. It's true that not every egg produces a chicken, but to leave the counting till later defies the spirit of faith and expectancy. You will never find an expectant mother shopping for cots and prams after the birth of a child – she's already done it because she is expectant.

George Müller, who housed thousands of young orphans in the late 1800s in Bristol, England, had a catch-phrase: "Expect great things from God and great things you will have". He saw God provide in powerful

Expect great things from God and great things you will have

65

ways throughout his life. On one occasion, when the orphanage had run out of food and it was time for breakfast, George Müller said to a young girl, "Come and see what the Father will do." He led her into a long dining room. There was nothing on the table except for empty dishes. The children were there, awaiting the first meal of the day. George Müller lifted his hands and prayed, "Dear Father, we thank Thee for what Thou art going to give us to eat." Shortly afterwards, there was a knock on the door. The baker stood there. "Mr Müller," the baker said, "I couldn't sleep last night. Somehow I felt that you didn't have breakfast and the Lord wanted me to send you some. So, I got up at two o'clock and baked some fresh bread, and I've brought it." Almost immediately afterwards there was a second knock on the door. This time it was the milkman, who announced that his milk cart had broken down outside and that he would like to give the children the cans of fresh milk, so that he could empty his wagon and repair it.[1]

Great expectations

Expectation is a vital component of the faith package. Early in Elijah's ministry he was met by a woman whose husband had died, and the debt collectors were set to take her sons as slaves in payment of the debts she owed them (2 Kings 4:1–7). Elijah told her to gather as many vessels from her neighbours' houses as possible. He specifically told her not to collect just a few. I suspect she filled up her lounge, kitchen and half her bedroom with jars and then, through tiredness, stopped. She was then instructed to pour out the jar of oil that she had left. As she did, the oil just kept on flowing. A miracle was happening before her eyes. When all the vessels were full, it was only then that the oil stopped flowing. The amount of oil she now had was in direct proportion to the amount of vessels she had collected. You could say, "according to her pots be it unto her." If she had collected more, she would have had more. If she had collected fewer, she would have had less. What she planned for, she got. She got the chickens because she counted them before they hatched.

Jesus said to the woman who had been bleeding for twelve years, "Your faith has healed you" (Matthew 9:22). Everyone was touching Jesus but only one was expectant. She got her healing because she expected her healing. It was the only miracle done behind Jesus' back, to prove that it was by faith alone and not through favouritism. She expected and she got. The nature of healthy, powerful, Christian living is to listen, to expect, to plan and to see. Most Christians say, "I believe God is able to do far more than I could ever ask or imagine." Faith says, "I *expect* God to do far more than I could ever ask or imagine."

A number of years ago, when our church needed a large sum of money to pay for the renovation of our building, we decided to have a faith-goal of £60,000. We invited the church to take part in the realisation of such an awesome target. Three weeks later on a Sunday morning we were amazed as we took up the money and the pledges. We found the total to be £60,017. Somebody had given seventeen pounds too much!

> Faith says, "I expect *God to do far more than I could ever ask or imagine"*

We've been expecting you

One day Jenny and I went to a large shopping centre to buy a watch. It was during the time when we had just come out of

Bible college and we were financially challenged. We were trusting and expecting God to do something good. We looked round the jewellers' and our eyes fell upon a beautiful gold Swiss watch. The watch was in a sale, so we thought that it might be 50% off. We were blown out to find that it was 90% less than its original retail price. We asked the assistant if it was a mistake, but, although she was mystified, she assured us it was correct and went ahead with the sale. We had expected blessing and we weren't disappointed. Jen was certainly keen to raise her hands in church *that* week!

I am expecting and planning for much growth in our church. We have built an auditorium much larger than is currently necessary, but it is in anticipation of what we expect will happen. In fact, the slogan of our church is "We've been expecting you!" It came about at a time when some good people were leaving our church. God led me to declare one Sunday to all the new people who had recently joined us, "We've been expecting you!" It was the start of a significant turnaround.

The movie *Field of Dreams* is all about a fantasy baseball team made up of all the best players from the past. The character played by Kevin Costner is urged by a voice from on high to build a stadium to house the "game of all games". The voice declares, "Build it and they will come." That is how God wants us to live as Christians.

Prophetic living is to stretch your tent curtains wide in anticipation of growth (Isaiah 54:2). Prophetic living is to push out into the deep for an anticipated catch. Count your chickens and expect great things to hatch. Break free of the conservatism that keeps the church of God small and weak. Let's expect great things and make today a preparation for a brilliant tomorrow.

A BIRD IN THE HAND IS ONLY WORTH HALF AS MUCH AS TWO IN THE BUSH

"Now if Robbie would like to put yesterday's chewing gum back under the desk we can all share Amy's birthday cake."

They say that a bird in the hand is worth two in the bush. Think about it – two available birds in the bush are actually worth *twice* as much as just one in the hand! Every person who has seen God do great things in their life and ministry has gone for the two in the bush. They simply have had the courage to let go of the one bird in the hand.

Life has two choices: keep what you've got and get no more, or be willing to lose what you've got and get much more. The Bible is loaded with examples of this powerful truth. A woman with a little bit of oil and flour was challenged by Elijah to give it all up. In place of it, she got a never-ending supply of oil and flour (1 Kings 17). David's mighty men were willing to give up their lives to serve their king, and because of it they saw some awesome victories (2 Samuel 23).

Jim Elliot was a missionary who attempted to contact and influence a South American tribe that had no previous contact with the West. After dispersing gifts from a helicopter, he attempted physical contact. Jim and his team were all brutally killed. It sparked grief and disbelief right across the United States that such a thing could happen in the 1960s. A reporter asked Jim's wife about her husband's death in the jungle; she replied: "Jim didn't die in the jungle, he died by his bed in high school when he gave his heart and soul to the service of Christ." His death sparked a great movement of God amongst the unreached tribes.

Hillsong Church in Sydney, Australia, has seen great numerical growth as well as astounding international influence through its senior minister, Brian Houston, and worship pastor, Darlene Zschech. Rarely has one church had such a significant impact. However, it all started when Frank Houston, Brian's dad, obeyed a call of God in 1977 to leave a thriving ministry in New Zealand and head for the "preachers' graveyard", Sydney. He left his country and people to attempt a great thing in God. Out of "death" has come incredible "life" that now pulses across the world.

Funeral for a friend

Jesus was clear when He said that whoever tries to "save his life will lose it, but whoever loses his life for my sake will save it" (Luke 9:24). Resurrection power only comes out of a good funeral. If you see a saint revelling in the capture of two birds in the bush, track back a little and you will see a funeral that took place when they let go of what they had in their hand. In your life you will sow tears and pain, but they will activate the switch that is needed to put the promise of Psalm 126:5–6 into operation: "Those who sow in tears will reap with songs of joy. He who goes out weeping, carrying seed to sow, will return with songs of joy, carrying sheaves with him."

Resurrection power only comes out of a good funeral

In the early 1990s, after the success of their performance during the interval of the Dublin-hosted Eurovision Song Contest, the *Riverdance* stage show was born. It launched Michael Flatley, a relatively unknown dancer and musician from Chicago, into the limelight. After consistent rave reviews and packed houses, the production company refused to offer Michael all he was looking for financially, so he decided to form his own dance company and launched the spectacular *Lord of the Dance*. To do it, he had to invest all that he had made from *Riverdance,* which meant he stood to lose millions. His story is one of many that go for the two birds in the bush. It is a natural law as well as a spiritual one.

Lose your life and you'll find it

Jesus said, "I tell you the truth, unless an ear of wheat falls to the ground and dies, it remains only a single seed. But if it dies, it produces many seeds. The man who loves his life will lose it, while the man who hates his life in this world will keep it for eternal life" (John 12:24–25). Often we try to avoid death and sacrifice, yet it is altars that God sets fire to and funerals where God raises the dead. For a farmer, sowing may appear to be a losing business. He can no longer see the grain when it has been sown because it is scattered in fields of dirt. It might look like a barren field but it is filled with potential. He waits for the harvest. Many people I know are too scared to let go of their seed and trust in the law of sowing and reaping. They want to hang onto their reputation, comforts, money, relationships and all manner of things. There is, however, no other way to the harvest than to let go, lay it down and give it up.

My wife was born in Queensland, Australia, where the weather is "beautiful one day, perfect the next". It is not just a tourist officer's slogan, it's the truth! After doing five years' full-time youth pastoring, God called us to England. We had seen the Hillsborough football stadium disaster in 1989 – an unprecedented tragedy in which around 100 people lost their lives. The events prompted us to think about the north of England, and we happened to end up in the very city where the Hillsborough stadium is situated – Sheffield. The weather in the north is not good. Drizzle is excessive and cloud cover is almost continuous. When my son Ryan was about three, I am convinced he was actually referring to the sun when he looked up and said, "What's that, Daddy?" In the first few years of living in Sheffield, I was starting to get a little agitated over my wife's problem with the new weather conditions she was living in. One day I read about Abraham. It said that God called him to leave his people, his father's house and his country to go to an unknown land (Genesis 12:1). His country was everything familiar to him: the scenery, the smells, and possibly the sunshine! I understood for the first time the great cost that my wife was paying to come to this new land. Much of the seed of sacrifice still lies in the soil, and even though we have seen a measure of harvest, much of it is yet to be seen!

For some of you it is time to let go of the bird in the hand. God has been challenging you to go for the two in the bush. The cost is great and the decision is big, but the outcome will be bigger than you have ever seen or dreamed of. Why not let go today and expect our creative God to take that seed in the dirt and convert it into tomorrow's reward?

KEEP GOING OVERBOARD

"Bother, I forgot the pickle again . . . Peter?!!"

They say do not go overboard. Going overboard is a must for any believer. Moderation and faith are arch-enemies. Faith is only activated in deep water. That is why Jesus said to Peter, "Put out into deep water, and let down the nets for a catch" (Luke 5:4). Miracles never happen in the shallows. It is only when you can't see the bottom and there's no turning back that faith is activated. The common ingredient to every miracle that occurred in the Bible is that the recipients found themselves in impossible situations. Impossibility is the soil in which divine possibility can germinate.

> *Impossibility is the soil in which divine possibility can germinate*

The point of no return

World War Two pilots knew with sobriety the expression "past the point of no return". The pilots relied on eyesight for navigation and in poor conditions often found themselves many miles from their target position with a full load of bombs on board and a tank of petrol that was on the "half-empty" mark. They had to make a definite decision whether or not to go past the point of no return. In other words, to pin-point their target and achieve their mission, they would forfeit the ability to return home. Going overboard is the only way to achieve the mission that God has for you.

Many people wonder why God leaves his breakthroughs until the eleventh hour. We often blame God, yet it wasn't until five to midnight that we let go of our final alternative and found ourselves completely abandoned to the hand of God. "If he doesn't come through . . . we're dead!" At 10 p.m. we had four options if God didn't come through. At 11 p.m. we had two and at 11:50 we still had a little nest egg we could turn to if God failed to come through.

It was in my first month at Bible college that I first started to give away large lumps of money. God was challenging me to offload a lot of the savings that I'd got together while working for two years as a plant manager for a concrete company. He wanted me to learn first-hand what it was to walk by faith for finance. He pushed me further and further into the deep. The following year I went deeper still. I had decided to work voluntarily for the church doing high school evangelism. We had come to the point where the pantry was totally depleted and I was depending on some money that would come from a little bit of maths tuition I was doing that day. I was looking forward to some money at the end of the teaching session but halfway through, the mother of the student apologised for not being able to pay that day. I was taken aback. After the lesson had finished and I was on my way out with nothing in hand, she suddenly stopped me. She said that while I was tutoring she had baked a pizza and made a cake for Jen and myself. I was amazed. I took them gladly and, upon returning home, raced up the garden path, opened the door and slipped the pizza under Jenny's knife and fork as she sat ready to eat by faith! It was God's provision – His daily bread for two people in deep water. God has not stopped providing since!

I remember another occasion when God came through, this time on a larger scale. After being in England for six years, Jen and I felt challenged to sell our house and move down market, releasing money for new plans for our church's expansion. We did it gladly and moved to an older house worth much less than the new one we had sold. Three years later, we sold our little house. We had a price war going on and the sale price kept rising and rising. Eventually, it sold for the same value as the previous house we had gladly given up. We had stepped out, going overboard in our service for God and His kingdom. We trusted Him over our financial future and He didn't let us down. In fact, our going overboard affected far more than just property. It made an incredible impact on my father's life. He encountered a working faith that was more than intellectual, above all logic and driven by a cause that was greater than our own lives. It was a "line in the sand" that challenged my father till the end of his life.

All eggs – one basket

They say don't put all your eggs in one basket; so that if that basket falls, you'll still have eggs remaining. But that's merely human wisdom. When faith is involved, only one basket is necessary. There's no back-up plan, no safety net. Why do miracles abound in Third World countries? It's because they rely solely upon God. When hospitals are inadequate, desperate people turn to God for healing. When wages are a pittance or non-existent, God is their source of supply. People in deep water have only one salvation, one solution, and one way forward: God. He's the strength in their human weakness, and He can be ours.

One day, a man went into heaven and was greeted by Peter at the gate. He wondered what the mountain of boxes contained that were piled up to the east of the courtyard. Peter told him that they were all "unclaimed miracles" that were destined for earth. Shrugging his shoulders, he said that they were ready to be given freely to those who got past *the point of no return*.

No more lifelines

I remember when I gave away all my Civil Engineering notes and books to a first-year student (who thought all his birthdays had come at once). To me it was a clear statement that I wasn't going back to the career I had chosen as an eighteen-year-old. God had now called me into the ministry and it was onwards and upwards for me! Some people keep pictures of old flames; some keep contact with members of an old church they used to go to. Even though it's called "love" and "fellowship", it is often really an extra security precaution, just in case things don't go too well in the deep waters of faith.

When one Hollywood lover gets their future wife or husband to take out a pre-nuptial agreement, you can almost guarantee the sinking of that relationship. Even human faith and trust fails if there's a life-raft waiting in the wings. Someone once said, "either He's the Lord of all, or He's not Lord at all." It's a paradox to "partly" trust in God, or make him 90% "Lord of your life". Either you believe God or you don't. Either you've got faith or you haven't. You cannot only "half believe". You can like the idea of something, but this is not to say that you necessarily believe. The Amplified Bible describes that "to believe in Christ" is to be *fully* reliant" upon Him. "Fully" means stepping out into miracle territory, walking on the water and being so transfixed by God's ability to provide that you don't need a lifeline. Back-up plans reduce faith to mere optimism.

Back-up plans reduce faith to mere optimism

Maybe for you it is time to step out of your boat and let the past be past; time to put the past behind and totally look to the future. Get rid of that lifeline! A man lost his sight and went for an operation. In coming out of the operating theatre he found that he had regained his sight but lost his memory. After another operation, he had regained his memory but lost his sight again. The surgeons concluded that he had to choose which one he wanted the most. The man said that it was an easy decision, he'd rather have his sight. He told the surgeon that "I'd rather see where I'm going than remember where I have come from."

Once, Dave Shearman from Nottingham Christian Centre prayed over me that I'd be given a "forward memory". This meant an ability not to recall the disappointments of the past, but to recall the prophetic word of the Lord, regularly, in my heart. The word "revision" doesn't just refer to a going-over of things that have already taken place. Spiritually it refers to a going-over of things *yet* to take place, a re-envisioning, going over the vision one more time.

Don't allow the enemy of your faith to hold you back with conservative, well-balanced Christianity. Christianity is a totally abandoned, totally excessive and totally exclusive day out with the Lord Jesus Christ. It is good to go out on a limb for that's where the rewards are. Let's go over the top by going overboard, and achieve great things for God!

DON'T BE YOURSELF

"But darling, I will be that size by the time we're on holiday."

They say, "Be yourself." I say, "Don't!" At times when I'm a little nervous and about to speak to a group of people, the last words of advice from my wife are usually, "Just be yourself!" I know what she means, but, for me, to be nervous *is* to be myself!

I find it difficult to answer personality profile tests largely because I'm evolving! There's submerged talent I never knew I had that's beginning to emerge. There are skills I'm developing that help me to manage areas I'm not naturally talented in, and there are areas of weakness that God has chosen to establish His strength and glory in. In Paul's letter to the Corinthians, he quotes Jesus' words to them: "My grace is sufficient for you, for my power is made perfect in weakness" (2

Corinthians 12:9). He goes on to say, "When I am weak, then I am strong." God's power and anointing is released at our weakest points. That is what our testimony is all about: when we couldn't, He could! God makes sure that we come to the end of ourselves – to the end of our own human strength – in order for us to break through into His power.

Crushed olives

One day a preacher came to our church in Australia and simply said to me, in front of the church, "Crushed olives." Although many of the congregation probably thought he was holding me responsible for the church buffet, his words meant something far more divine to me! The Holy Spirit was breaking me down and crushing me in order to get the oil of God to flow out of my life.

The most powerful sermons that a minister ever gives are the ones where God has placed great power on an area of great weakness. That's their revelation, their testimony. I often talk about the affirmation of God and His favour and pleasure towards us. Where does this come from? It comes from a real lack of affirmation in my upbringing and from self-doubt, plaguing every move I used to make. I now know God as my closest supporter.

What about you? What are the current areas in your personality that are under divine reconstruction? And what are the things He's already done? As you follow His leading, don't focus on what you *used* to be like; begin to focus on who you are *becoming*! God is doing a good work in you and He'll be faithful to complete it (Philippians 1:6).

The two of you

There is another way of discussing all of this. In you are two
people: the old you and the new you. In fact, you are a mixture
of both. The more you change, the more new there is and the
less old there is. One evening I was sitting with my wife in our
lounge. I was in a bad mood and the phone rang. I answered
it and found it to be a member of our congregation. Suddenly,
my whole demeanour changed. I was bright, charming and
very likeable! When I put down the phone, I was told that I
should become an actor, I was so good at "putting it on". The
truth was that both the bad-mood man and the good-mood
man were me. The good-mood man was not a fake. According
to Romans chapter 6, the impostor was the bad-mood man. It
was that man who was crucified with Christ. Paul urges us to
reckon ourselves dead to sin. In other words, to place our lives
in line with the knowledge that the sinful man no longer has
a hold on us. We are no longer slaves to the sinful man, thanks
to Jesus' death and resurrection. We may still be sinning, but
the masterstroke is that we don't have to. When Abraham
Lincoln declared freedom for the slaves in 1865, many still
stayed on the farms they had been working on for years. The
reason was twofold – for some, nobody told them they were
now free. For others, they knew no other life, and even though
freed they continued to serve their master's wishes. When
you were born again the chains of sin fell off and you were no
longer held in darkness. All that is needed is for you to walk
out of the jail. Ephesians chapter 4 tells us to put off the old
man and put on the new man. To be yourself is to die to the
old man and live as the new.

Paul himself wrestled with the sinful nature. In Romans

chapter 7 he explains, "I do not understand what I do. For what I want to do I do not do, but what I hate to do. And if I do, what I do not want to do, I agree that the law is good. As it is, it is no longer I myself who do it, but it is sin living in me" (Romans 7:15–17).

G.K. Chesterton's fictitious detective, Father Brown, solved his cases by imagining himself in the minds of his murderers. "You may think a crime was horrible because you could never commit it," he said to a questioner. "I think it is horrible because I could commit it."[1] We are all potential criminals! Jesus was tempted in every way that we are, but He showed us a victorious way. Paul concluded his chapter by crediting Jesus for his victories. Here are four ways to help you be the self that God wants you to be:

Exercise the power of choice

The power to choose is one of the most underrated powers in the church

The power to choose is one of the most underrated powers in the church. We constantly blame the devil for the things he only tempted us to do. He didn't do it – *we* did it! I can imagine the devil with a growing ego, taking all the credit for our mistakes. To "put on" and "put off" is the language of choice. It says: you choose!

Feed the new man

One day a tormented man went to see a psychologist and told him his problem. "Every day I see two dogs fighting," he lamented. "A black dog and a white dog." The psychologist was interested. He inquired whether one particular dog would win the fight. The tormented man replied, "Yes. The one I feed the most." The more you feed on the word of God, the more you exercise the new man within you, and the stronger he gets. The less time you spend feeding and exercising the old man, the weaker he gets. Have you ever noticed that before a television movie ever gets to the bedroom scene, you get a strong impression that one is approaching? To the vision-led Christian, the bedroom scene is wrong to watch. Jesus clearly said that to look at a woman lustfully is matched with the sin of adultery (Matthew 5:28). Before any bedroom scene takes place on the screen, the feeding plan of your inner man is in operation. The film begins to exercise the old man minutes before you have even arrived at the sinful scenes. You find yourself carried along with the movie, like a boat being led by the current. Bizarrely, you find yourself wanting a relationship with the leading man or the leading lady – even though each is already married to another person. Why is that? It is because the old, sinful man likes not only to be exercised but also to be fed. If you feel that you just cannot help yourself when it comes to sin, it is because you have fed the old man too often. It is wisdom not to put yourself in places of temptation. Window-shopping may not be genuine shopping, but it eventually leads to inside shopping. If you play on slippery riverbanks, you are likely to fall in!

Don't stick up for the old man!

Paul says, "What a wretched man I am! Who will rescue me from this body of death?" (Romans 7:24). He called a spade a spade; his old self he called "wretched". Sometimes we need to magnify sins and not disguise them. You can only really appreciate grace when you see how much you deserve judgement. John Newton, who was captain of a slave ship, realised the full magnitude of his sin when he penned "Amazing grace, how sweet the sound that saved a wretch like me".

It is time to put on the wig, become the judge and condemn all sin within your life. Don't stick up for it. Some say, "That's just the way I am." Sometimes we even grade sin. I remember at university we thought smoking was okay in comparison to all the injustices committed across the globe. Sometimes our culture legitimises certain sins by making documentaries about them, thereby allowing society to enjoy the sin through the back door! Rather than put films on television called "Strip Club" or "Lap-dancing Bonanza", producers make "documentaries" about these issues. Documentaries are our voyeuristic way of sinning but not feeling so guilty.

The first key to repentance and to letting the new man reign within us is to acknowledge our sin. Admission is the starting point of a turn from sin to righteousness. If we defend ourselves when we are wrong, we will find ourselves caught in the jail from which we were once freed.

Count yourself dead to sin

Paul writes, "In the same way, count yourself dead to sin but alive to God in Christ Jesus" (Romans 6:11). By faith, we are dead to sin. It is not by feelings but by faith. Do the count – you are dead to sin. There is no condemnation any longer. Deal with any sinful behaviour and at the same time stand upon the conquests of Christ. Apply the cross and the resurrection and count on it. You were dead, but now you are alive.

Be the self you are becoming! Be the brand-new you that is made in the image of Christ. Be the person that is being transformed from glory into glory. It's amazing to know that we're not who we thought we were!

#11

ROLLING STONES CAN STILL GATHER MOSS

"I don't mind the moss, it's the gum, cigarette butts & ring-pulls that really turn me over."

They say a rolling stone gathers no moss, yet there are a lot of stones that both roll and gather moss! A stone that rolls down a mossy hill picks up the moss that it rolls through – it cannot help it. It is a product of its environment. Similarly, we are a product of our environment. Why is it that Richard Branson is the UK's foremost entrepreneur? There must be a link between his life and those of his grandmother, who was the oldest lady in the world to get a hole in one at golf, and his mother, who made money from selling home-made boxes to Harrods.[1] Chris Bonington is the UK's most acclaimed mountaineer and the first British climber to ascend the south-west face of Everest. Is it just self-motivation that has given him the drive, or is it something to do with the facts that his dad is one of the founding members of the SAS and two of his great-great-grandfathers struck gold at the Great Australian Gold Rush in the 1800s?[2] The environment in which it exists has a lot to do with what a stone collects.

Creating a champion culture

If the environment or culture in which you develop can hold such a sway over the outcomes of life, and it is your heart that determines the future (Proverbs 4:23), it's a smart move to place your heart in an environment that will encourage it to prosper. David's victory over Goliath wasn't all that difficult. In fact, he simply ran towards him, flung one smooth stone and the giant fell down one stone heavier! David didn't become a champion after defeating Goliath; he already *was* a champion. He had created a champion culture around his life that produced a champion heart, which produced champion results. He didn't win in life just because of his calling to become king. In fact, his selection was down to the fact that he had a heart for God and a heart like God's (1 Samuel 13:14; 1 Samuel 16:7). David created a champion culture by developing three essential things in his life:

He developed a strong conviction

A conviction is something that you uncompromisingly stand upon. It is the belief that will stand the pressures of circumstances and the heat of the battle. 1 Samuel 17:40 says, "Then *he* took *his* staff in *his* hand, chose five smooth stones from the stream, put them in the pouch of *his* shepherd's bag, and, with *his* sling in *his* hand, approached the Philistine."

Firstly, David had a conviction in his call. He had a confidence in who he was that caused him to gather up his tools and approach the giant. Look at the number of times this one verse refers to David himself. When his brother Eliab accused him of wrong motives, David brushed him off with the confidence of his call.

Secondly, David had the conviction of his history. His staff, his bag and his sling represented his past life as a shepherd. They also represented some past successes that had prepared him for this time. He had killed the lion and the bear, and these success stepping stones proved an undeniable history. When his leader Saul tried to intimidate him by calling him "only a boy" (1 Samuel 17:33), David's convictions knew that this was true in terms of age, but not in terms of experience. When someone asks me how long it takes to prepare a sermon, I often say ten to twenty years. A woman once met Picasso in a restaurant and asked him to draw something on her napkin. She said that she would pay for the privilege. Picasso responded with a request for $10,000. "But, you did that in only 30 seconds," the woman exclaimed. "No," Picasso retorted, "It has taken me 40 years to do that." Your whole Christian walk is preparation for a day like today. Most people feel as if they are a product of how the last week has been or how much time they have spent in prayer over the last month. The truth is, our history goes much further back. All of us have notches on our staff to past conquests of lions and bears. It is time to check the notches and get a conviction that we are building on a strong foundation.

Thirdly, David had a conviction of his source. He knew that it wasn't so much by the sling or staff that the Lord saves, but by the power of God. It was his conviction that it was God's power that made his stones so deadly. He refused to wear the restrictive armour of the day. He refused to let the old, worn-out methods blunt his God-given ability. Religion is defined when methods become more important than the purpose. For every new season in God, there are always new methods, but we need to realise that it's God who gives success, and not the method.

He developed strong commitment

You can have great convictions of the heart but, unless the commitments in your mind line up, you'll find that life will let you down. Your entire course of action comes from your entire course of thinking. As I've said before, it's not just what you believe that ultimately counts, it's what you *think* about what you believe.

David was committed to today's success. He had mastered the lion and the bear and he wasn't waiting for his "big opportunity". I remember a Bible college student ringing me up in order to tell me that he couldn't make it to one of our Sunday services because of difficulties in the necessary travel arrangements. He did add, however, that he could possibly have made it if he had been preaching. Bad confession! A lot of people are looking for the lucky break. Paul Daniels, a popular UK entertainer in the 1990s, was asked about his concept of "luck". He said that luck was really "when years of preparation meet a moment of opportunity". I also heard the comment that "if opportunity isn't knocking, build a door!".

If opportunity isn't knocking, build a door!

He was committed to the follow-through

David was faithful to his father's sheep. To Eliab, his brother, they were just a few straggly sheep in the desert. To David, they were his chief concern. He was faithful to his talents, so much so that he ended up being a harp player in the king's palace. Reliability is the pool from which God selects his champions. Paul's instruction to Timothy was to select "reliable men" to train and rub off on, so they can do the same (2 Timothy 2:2).

He developed a strong confession

What you say will have a big impact on the culture or environment that you create. The Bible says that "the tongue has the power of life and death" (Proverbs 18:21). You may have a strong conviction and commitment, but you can still be dogged by a faltering confession. David established a powerful confession. He declared to the giant, "This day the Lord will hand you over to me, and I will strike you down and cut off your head" (1 Samuel 17:46). At times, confession can be prophetic and can actually create your God-given future, but at other times, good confession produces the heat that fills the hothouse, the growth-fuel that feeds the seeds of success.

The greatest faith-word in the Old Testament is the word "but". It is a word that acknowledges the current situation, then added a previously unconsidered fact that changes everything. David used it in Psalm 31. He saw himself as forgotten, broken and conspired against, and then added the great faith word "but". "But I trust in you, O LORD; I say, 'You are my God'" (Psalm 31:14). Faith confronts reality, it doesn't deny it. Great confession acknowledges the current situation and then slam-dunks it with previously unconsidered truth. Abraham faced the fact that his body was past its use-by date, "yet he did not waver through

Faith confronts reality, it doesn't deny it

unbelief regarding the promise of God" (Romans 4:20). David saw the uncircumcised Philistine yet witnessed his downfall.

If you want to be a rolling stone that gathers speed and not moss, it is important to create a culture that promotes just that. Your convictions of the heart, commitments of the mind and confession of the mouth will create a culture that has the capacity to turn all of its potential into fast-moving, moss-eliminating action. More power to you!

START TEACHING OLD DOGS
NEW TRICKS

"Don't you just hate smart alecs?"

They say you can't teach an old dog new tricks. I say you can and you should. Old is not an age; it's an attitude. You can be 75 and have the attitude of a 25-year-old, and you can be 25 and have the attitude of someone who is 75. Jesus said that no one puts new wine into old wineskins or else the wineskins may crack open and the wine be lost (Matthew 9:14–17). An old wineskin was characterised by its lack of elasticity – its inability to adapt. What makes an old person young at heart? Surely it is their ability to adapt to new situations and be taught new tricks. The moral of good Christian living is never to grow old.

Colonel Sanders founded his fried-chicken fast-food chain

at the age of 65. My mother found herself divorced in her early fifties and resolved to go back to school. After failing a law degree, she completed an arts degree and then went back to the law school. In her mid-sixties she set up her own law practice and sold it in her early seventies. She may have been "old" but she didn't stop learning new tricks!

The bell curve

The three-stage bell curve of the growth and decline of a business is well known. The youth stage is characterised by high innovation, high enthusiasm and a strong sense of destiny and purpose. The mid-life stage is characterised by high levels of strategy, good practice and good control. The old-age stage begins when enthusiasm dies, new ideas are resisted and the "we do it" is the commander-in-chief instead of "*why* we do it". Doctor Al Bernard, a New York minister, has rightly added a fourth stage – death! The best thing to do when you've died is to realise it! Then you can set yourself up for a possible resurrection.

The challenge for every human is to stay young, stay innovative, stay adaptable and stay spiritual. Never forget the cause! Never lose sight of what you're fighting for. Two men looked out from prison bars – one saw mud and the other saw the stars. Be the one who always sees the stars and reaches out for them. I remember a minister sitting down in my office and saying that when I first came to the city of Sheffield it caused quite an uproar. The new kid in town with the church called "The Hope of Sheffield Christian Church" certainly seemed to have an inflated belief in his sense of purpose and destiny. He said he was pleased that now so many speak well of me and that my integration into city church life seems complete. I managed to hold back my response for about ten minutes while others talked. Then I responded to his observation with a note of concern. To me, some negative reaction is a sure sign that you're still young and vital. Many times, disturbances are a sign of a new idea and a fresh initiative. The wild behaviour that comes from human insecurity is easily provoked when old ways of thinking are confronted head-on by new thinking and new ways of doing things. Jesus ate at many barbecues supplied by the finest holy cows! The new wineskin of relationship with God stood in direct confrontation with the old wineskins of Jewish Law.

The freshness factor

Another characteristic of new things is "freshness". There's nothing like fresh bread or fresh fruit. I remember once cycling around New Zealand and coming to a place called Queenstown. Being hungry, I devoured an entire freshly-made loaf of bread. My mouth still begins to water when I recall its warm aroma. Bread that is a few days old is still the same stuff, but it's lost a vital quality: its freshness. Hillsong Music, from the Hillsong Church in Sydney, has been a great international success story. Many of the songs have become classics and are sung across the globe. Someone once asked Brian Houston, who pastors Hillsong Church, how long he felt it would all last. Brian's reply was, "As long as we stay fresh."

Bob Hope once said, "You know you're getting old when the candles cost more than the cake." May that be the only side of old age that you experience in your life and ministry. Stay inventive, stay teachable, stay in touch with your culture, keep on the edge and most of all – stay fresh. Keep learning new tricks!

IT MAY TAKE TWO TO TANGO, BUT IT ONLY TAKES ONE TO FOXTROT

"Show off!"

They say it takes two to tango. The tango is one of the rare dances that take two people to accomplish. It may take two to tango, but I say it only takes one to dance alone and break away from the pack and create a whole new way of doing things. Never underestimate the power of one. God called one man to deliver millions from the dictatorial grip of Pharaoh. God called one man to take five smooth stones and slay Goliath. God called one man to rebuild the broken-down walls of Jerusalem after its fall to Babylon. God always selects one person. Throughout the Bible, he gives the vision and strategy to one person, and then gathers a team together to work out the vision. It takes great courage to be different and go where no man has been before. If Karl Benz had not broken away from the horse and carriage he would never have invented the world's first horseless carriage. If George Biro had not broken away from the inflexible fountain pen, he never would have invented the world's first ballpoint. Had the Blanket brothers of Bristol not broken away from skins and rugs, we would never have enjoyed the snugness of the blanket. If the fourth Earl of Sandwich had been happy to stop his card game for a sit-down lunch, we would never have experienced the convenience of the sandwich. Each of these people defied convention; they were prepared to do what had never been done before and try out a new way of doing things.

In 1517, a German monk called Martin Luther nailed a list of 95 complaints about the corrupt state of the church to the door of Wittenberg Church in Germany. He marked the beginning of the Reformation. He was branded a heretic and a rebel. In today's language he would perhaps have been labelled a "lone ranger", but, despite the stigma, he changed the course of history. He danced alone and caused a revolution.

No more status quo

Stop waiting for others to "get it" and start to launch out into the world of thought that you've been incubating. When you put your head above the parapet, you'll always endure criticism and abuse. People will often tolerate dreamers, but they will not tolerate those who dare to live their dream. It reminds them of the dreams that have been left dormant for years within their lives. It challenges their ways and confronts their comfy world.

The Gilpin family tree has a history of challenging convention. The Gilpin coat of arms features a wild boar. Apparently, around the beginning of the thirteenth century, Richard Degylpin slew a wild boar that had been terrorising the neighbourhood. For this act of courage he was given land and a manor house in the English Lake District. In the sixteenth century, Bernard Gilpin stood up against the state of the church and narrowly escaped death at the Tower of London. He was known as the Apostle of the North. In the twentieth century, in Australia, Alan Gilpin – my father – stood up against the Victoria government's nonchalant attitude towards the horrific pollution caused by giant corporate industry. He didn't escape getting sacked from a prestigious job as chairman of Australia's foremost environmental agency and, today, many breakthroughs have come from his willingness to dance alone.

People will often tolerate dreamers, but they will not tolerate those who dare to live their dream

Mal Fletcher, who leads a European youth movement called Next Wave International, defines a leader as "someone who challenges the status quo and points the way to something better". They are not simply critics, but gap-finders and solution-makers. Maybe you're like me and you don't seem to fit the box. When your time is right in God, launch out and give it a go. If you win – congratulations! If you fall back into the tango then at least you gave it a go.

Failure is a good option

I'm convinced that God will reward me not only for my successes, but also for many of my failures! He'll say to

Gabriel – "Another crown for Gilpin," and I'll say "But, Lord, I tried and failed." He'll then say "That failure, Dave, was a sign of a great attempt!" Sometimes we get things wrong, but if our motivation is right, then our initiative will be honoured. Peter may have stepped out onto the water and sunk, but at least he stepped out – which is more than can be said for the other eleven! Tom Hanks is one of Hollywood's biggest stars. He won great critical acclaim for both *Saving Private Ryan* and *Castaway*. *You've got Mail* hit all the right commercial buttons and became a huge hit when he co-starred with Meg Ryan. *Philadelphia* earned two Oscars back-to-back and *Apollo 13* earned him Academy Award nomination. But every success has had a backlog of failed attempts. Whoever remembers Tom Hanks in the *Money Kid*, or in *Volunteers*, or *Bonfire of the Vanities*? What about *Joe versus the Volcano*? Maybe, but in *Punchline*, certainly not![1]

Andrew Evans, formerly the leader of the Australian Assemblies of God Churches, said that success is doing the right thing for long enough. I love the idea of the learning curve. If you have failed, it means you can learn from it and be a better person for it. Jonathan Swift once said, "Never be ashamed to admit you have been wrong, 'tis but saying you are wiser today than you were yesterday."

Remember it takes two to tango, but only one to breakthrough. Sitting in jail in the American Deep South, Martin Luther King decided he could make a difference. He would no longer dance the dance of exploitation, as generations of his people had

> *Jonathan Swift once said, "Never be ashamed to admit you have been wrong, 'tis but saying you are wiser today than you were yesterday"*

done for so many years. This humble preacher took the initiative to lead an unprecedented non-violent revolution – a revolution that eventually raised so much awareness that the intangible dream of civil rights became a tangible reality. It took just one man to break through that ceiling, for millions of others to follow. One unlikely, ordinary, Christian man challenged the status quo and changed American society forever. Will *you* be that man; will *you* be that woman for your world? Will *you* dare to break free from the pack and attempt to be that gap-finder and that solution-maker? Go on – you only live once!

IT'S NEVER TWO STEPS FORWARD
AND ONE STEP BACK

"Taint fair! He's supposed to go back one now!"

They say, "It's two steps forward and one step back."
According to the word of God, life is never two steps forward
and one step back, unless you let it be so! You can create a
godly way of thinking that sees life as a continuous victory.
Either you're winning "out there" or you're winning in your
heart. Your territory of influence is being expanded outwardly,
or the territory of your heart is being enlarged inwardly. The
Bible tells us, "And we know that in all things God works for
the good of those who love Him, who have been called according to His purpose" (Romans 8:28). It doesn't say some things,
but *all* things. Everything. Life with God is always forward. He

has purpose in the rough times and, as we see ourselves as "always moving forwards", we begin to tap into how God sees our world, and that's great living.

The power of momentum

One of the secret underlying powers of life is the power of momentum. As we keep moving forwards, step by step, we gather it. The most powerful rivers of the

One of the secret underlying powers of life is the power of momentum

world such as the Ganges and the Mississippi aren't the fastest, yet, with a vast quantity of water being carried along, they are certainly in the running for being the most powerful. When you have momentum, you become increasingly unstoppable. As a kid it was easy to make a dam across one of the small creeks that ran near our house in Queensland, yet changing the course of a large river is another story completely!

Mathematically, momentum is created by depth multiplied by width, multiplied by length, multiplied by speed. Simply put, it is volume times velocity. To create momentum in your life, it will take more than running fast into destiny. It will also take both width of experience and depth of revelation. Undying passion plus a large heart is a powerful combination.

When life sends you a "one step back" kind of deal, it is your God-given opportunity to become both deeper and wider. God builds His ministry on proven faithfulness that doesn't quit when the going gets tough. He also builds His church on revelation. Revelation is the revealing of mysteries unknown to the natural mind. The best environment in which to receive

new depth of revelation is adversity! God
has secrets that He builds His church on. As
you call out for wisdom in the time of trial,
God will give you the stuff that causes you
to become an undeniable force for the
kingdom of God.

> *The best*
> *environment in*
> *which to*
> *receive new*
> *depth of*
> *revelation is*
> *adversity!*

The potter and the clay

When a potter seeks to make a vessel that will be used to pour
out water for the thirsty and medicine for the sick, he is aware
of seven essential processes:

He finds you and frees you

The potter must find some suitable clay. Most clay is unrec-
ognisable to the untrained eye, as the impurities can make it
look like mud. When God sees you, He sees your full potential. We see our weaknesses and our sin, but He sees our
strengths and His fullness. Michelangelo took a large piece of
marble and created the world's greatest statue – the statue of
David. Even though the marble had a fracture running
through it, he knew he could do something with it. He saw
the statue in the marble before he had created it. God sees
your future today in your present. After finding you and
freeing you from the kingdom of darkness, the potter then
puts the clay in the sack on his back and heads for the potter's
shed. It's a great feeling to be resting on the shoulder of the
Almighty God. Many Christians want to stay there forever;
they are passionate and hungry but have little depth and little
width. God wants to make vessels that will hold great capacities and not blow up in the kiln or break through constant

usage. To do this He must take you onto the next step in the process of creating a vessel that can be used mightily for His purposes.

He refines you

The potter now takes the clay and empties it from his bag onto the potter's bench and begins to break it open. "He who falls on this stone will be broken to pieces, but he on whom it falls will be crushed" (Matthew 21:44).

He will use circumstances to bring to the surface what is truly within you, creating a desperation to be cleansed and to be changed. Often we will find ourselves on the cross for something we never did. Sometimes we've done our best and it is simply not good enough. Maybe your best friend has turned and abandoned you in your time of need. It's a set up! It's an opportunity for a win – for a step forward. It's your chance to win on the inside, to see His love and sovereignty. It's your chance to trust more, to love more and to be more like Him. It's your chance to work with God as He digs out the roots of rebellion, independence and pride. God is an expert potter – be pliable in His hands! There are several things to remember during this part of the process.

a) Add more water!   The potter knows that water makes the process easier. It is the water of His word that will ease you in the time of pain. Read the Psalms. Ask God to reveal Himself to you. He will!

b) Never confuse God's testings with God's judgements.   God is not punishing you – He is making you. He is not far from you – He is with you. Like the coach of a football team, He is longing for you to succeed and is "an ever-present help in trouble" (Psalm 46:1).

c) Focus on God, and not the devil.   Many people blame the devil for so much that he never did. The devil is a pawn in the hand of God. Somebody once said that the devil is the grinding wheel that is used for our sharpening as God's chosen instrument. It is God who turns the grinding wheel. If the devil ever gets somebody to turn on you and disown you, then rejoice: God is making a winning situation for you. He wants you to take a step forward into the likeness of Christ. Don't focus on the devil or on circumstance, but give God praise and use it as an opportunity to know God's love and to exhibit God's love even when the enemy abounds.

d) Focus on the outcome and not the testing.   The tests that come from God are to create a positive outcome. James tells us that simply to stick it out during hard times produces a great harvest (James 1). The best is yet to come. If anyone takes anything away from you, know this – when God restores, He gives back far more than that which was taken away in the first place.

e) Live in the secret place.   There is a place hidden for those in trouble. The one who's never been there will never know where they are going when the tough times come. "For in the day of trouble He will keep me safe in His dwelling; He will hide me in the shelter of His tabernacle and set me high upon a rock" (Psalm 27:5). Someone once said, "Come apart before you come apart." It's your call.

He positions you

The next step in the process is that the potter positions you. He places you in the centre of His wheel – in the centre of His will. Positioning is everything. In Formula One it is everything; in tennis it is everything. With Elisha, getting the mantle of anointing from Elijah was everything. Being in the right place at the right time is a great secret of success.

If you're scared, do it scared

The centre of the wheel is often a scary place. It says, "Not my will but yours be done." It is a place where your hands are completely off the controls. Joyce Meyer once said, "If you're scared, do it scared." The centre of the wheel is a holy place, positioned at the centre of His attention.

He shapes you

When God begins to shape us there's a new sense of His hand being upon our life. Life with God regains its experiential edge and a sense of His hand seems firmly upon us. We sense His call again. We sense that we're now getting somewhere. Never stop the wheel in the middle of shaping. We look much better spinning. Be sure not to compare yourself with another who's on another wheel. We all have different personalities, gifts, callings and capacities. We also have different starting positions. Some of you are first-generation Christians. You are pioneers of the faith, pulling down the huge oak trees and paving the way for others to come and settle in the vast acres of territory that you have broken open for them. Some people are third- and fourth-generation Christians – of those to whom much is given, much is expected.

He heats you up

The kiln speaks of new resolution and new conviction. The heat is there to firm you up and not to destroy you. This is the place when the devil tries his hardest and you just say "no". It's where you're tempted to compromise and you simply fail to make adjustments for what you're doing. When the Sanballats of this world say "Come down and talk for a while" but you refuse to get off the wall because you know that this is where you're meant to be. When you make a resolution to not accept less than God's best.

He ignores you

One of the last steps in the process that a potter takes clay through is to leave you on the shelf for a short time of cooling down. This is the place where you notice other pots being used instead of you. People who have been Christians for less time than you, are being hand-selected for positions and roles that you ought to have got. People who are less mature than you are having doors of opportunity open up within their lives that you simply deserve. This process finally challenges you to consider what the whole thing is about – making you famous or making God famous? This is the time when you realise, like Joseph, that the dream was not for yourself, but for the deliverance of a nation. It doesn't matter who gets the glory as long as God is exalted and worshipped.

He paints you

The final step in the process is when the potter paints the pot. He gives you beauty for ashes. He restores your outward blessings. He gives you a good name that is more precious than gold or silver (Proverbs 22:1). Many potters would say that the greatest moment in their work is when the kiln is finally reopened and the colours and designs are seen in all their resplendent brilliance. For God, the Master Potter, the greatest time is not this at all! His greatest moment is when He releases His awesome power and invites you to be the vessel you were called to be. You are called to be a vessel of honour that brings refreshment to the weary and healing to the sick. You're a strong, large, capable vessel that has been fashioned by God, and is to be used to bring Jesus to the nations. You weren't born to be an ornament, but a vessel of honour, fit for the Master's use.

Victorious living is not two steps forward and one step back. It is two steps forward, one step forward, two steps forward – forever! It is a perpetual win-win situation. Time to rethink how many things work together for good for those who love God and live in His purposes. It could possibly be all things! Your life is in the hand of the Master Potter. There's no better place to be.

IT'S THE WINNING, NOT THE TAKING PART, THAT COUNTS

"So let's get out there team and really . . . er . . ."

They say it's not the winning but the taking part that counts. *Hello?* That's why there are so many bad teams! A team that lacks purpose and direction is no longer a team, but simply a group of people on a field. Without people working for one goal and one purpose, everybody works for their own goals and their own purposes. Someone once said, "Don't give me teamwork, give me a team that works." For a team to work, everybody must know why he or she is out on the field. Everybody must work in synergy to create corporate outcomes. Everybody must focus on the goal.

Creating a winning team

Without goals, people play for themselves. With goals, there's a chance to create a team in which people live and breathe both for each other and for results. Some teams are filled with people who love to get the ball and show off their talents, but they refuse to pass the ball on. They love the recognition and attention, but they have forgotten the very reason they are all out on the field. I love to create a team that is over the moon when anyone else scores a goal. When another scores, we all realise it is from our collective effort – the winnings are shared. The key to breaking this independent, fractionalising spirit is never to begin building with the trendy subject of "empowerment". The first role of every team member is not to be empowered but, through faithfulness and diligence, to empower the leader. When the goal of every person is the goal of the leader and their heart is set on doing all they can to help the team to score – you've got a winning team as well as a team that wins.

Empowerment should never be chapter one; it should always be a chapter that comes after the chapters on the heart – motive and attitude are more foundational than power. Releasing more power from the engine of a boat without a rudder to steer the ship in the right direction means certain disaster.

Serving another man's vision

Many leaders empower people far too early because of their own insecurity. It's tough standing head and shoulders above the rest, but that is the leader's call! Strong leadership and dictatorship may look similar, but are poles apart in both motive and operation. People who refuse to be made into team players will often accuse leadership of being dictatorial. Many leaders buckle under such accusations and then spend many years compromising their God-given vision to gain a life of peace. A dictator will force their hand to comply, but a strong leader waits until the right spirit of servanthood is found in the person, then places them on the team.

Joseph had a dream at a very young age. He dreamed that everyone in his family would one day bow down to him (Genesis 37:5–7). It was a God-given dream, but before he could move into it and see it come to pass, he actually had to learn to serve the dreams of others. Bought by Potiphar to be a slave in his household, he took the challenge to make it the most successfully run household in the neighbourhood. He fulfilled Potiphar's intention in buying him. When thrown into jail, he more than fulfilled the keeper of the jail's dream to have the place spick and span. He even took the dreams of the butler and the baker and helped them with divine inter-pretations. It has been said that if you become a fulfiller of another man's dream, God will give you your own. I only half go along with this. In fact, if you follow God's call to fulfil another man's dream totally, it will, for an appointed period, become your dream. You'll own the dream. One day, Brian Houston had a meeting with his assistant. His assistant shared his allegiance with Brian and said he wanted to get behind Brian's vision with everything that he had. Brian looked at him and said, "That's simply not good enough." His assistant was taken aback. Brian went on to say that he didn't want it to be his vision but *their* vision. I love it when the people of Hope City Church (formally The Hope of Sheffield

Christian Church – we changed our name a few years back) talk about "our vision". Often, vision isn't just what is written up on a business card or hanging off a board, it's everything that is deliberate about a place and a people. It is the language used as much as the community outreach programme. It's the enthusiasm as much as the education of the people. They say that vision is not caught but taught. I say it's both.

X-rays: no thanks

"Investors in People" is a national, government-recognised standard of excellence. We achieved it in the business sector of our church. One remark our assessor made was about the lack of public exposure for our vision statement. He asked why we didn't put our vision statement up in the entrance foyer of our centre. The fact is, when people meet me I don't hand them an X-ray of my bone structure. The bones are supporting me and the general size of my bones is evident to all, but it's the life around the bones that is the purpose of the skeletal structure. If you dig down into the life of our church, you'll find some clearly defined X-rays. But, to people who understand vision, it should be obvious what the vision is, through the environment and atmosphere that is generated around it. You can tell when there's bacon on the grill simply by its smell. You can tell when the lights are on simply by the colours they generate. Vision always gives itself away by its smell, its look and the sound that it creates!

Vision always gives itself away by its smell, its look and the sound that it creates!

If you want to be a real team player who will one day be empowered and released to exercise great authority, find a good leader and get sold on their vision and make it yours. In Australia, God called me to a church where the Senior Minister just loved country music. I knew it was God's church for me so I sank my life into its vision. Now there is one kind of music I dislike intensely – yes, you've guessed it – country music! Well, we got into it and eventually had fun doing it. Upon leaving to go to England, we sowed one of our largest offerings back into the place that we were departing from. Today, I feel incredibly empowered by God, and have an awesome team to support me. We're all playing for one vision and one goal. Jesus said this: "For whoever wants to save his life will lose it, but whoever loses his life for me will save it" (Luke 9:24).

Now if you're a team leader, don't be the only one with your eyes on the goal. I am regularly telling our team leaders that we're not here just for the fun – even though it *is* fun to be around each other – and we're not here just for the fellowship – even though we have some great times of friendship and camaraderie. We are here to extend the kingdom of God through the vision God has given to us. It is not simply playing the game that counts; we need to make it our goal to win, and accomplish all that God wants us to achieve.

A MILLION POUNDS FOR
YOUR THOUGHTS

They say, "A penny for your thoughts?" Some are worth millions! Your mind has the creative ability to spurn ideas that may change the world. No one has a mind quite like yours. When the chairman of Sony displayed the Sony Walkman to his board, no one believed in its marketability. The idea of going back to what looked like the old crystal radio with the earplugs was not where technology seemed to be heading. The chairman persisted with the product and the rest is history. The thought of a highly portable music system was worth millions. When Steve Jobs had the idea of taking out the complexity of inputting into computer programmes and replacing it with an on-screen format and a mouse, his thought was no less than revolutionary. It gave birth to the personal computer, and today it is the only way. Your thoughts could change the course of history and revolutionise your community. As a teenager, Matthew Barnett thought it would be good to have a church that was open 24 hours a day, seven days a week. At 20 years of age he went to Los Angeles to take on a small, dying pastorate. He noticed a large hospital up for sale, and knew that it was the place where God wanted to establish his 24/7 church. It had 1,738 rooms and eventually he bought it for 3.9 million dollars. Seven years later, the old hospital caters for two hundred ministries with over six hundred people ministering on the streets each day. Crime in the local area has dropped by 73%, so much so that President George W. Bush visited what is now called the Dream Center and claimed it to be a model project for the rest of the United States of America.

Read the sell-by date

It's time to challenge the way in which we think. Francis Bacon once said, "A prudent question is one half of wisdom."

> *Francis Bacon once said, "A prudent question is one half of wisdom"*

Asking "why" will challenge the "what". To get to the bottom of any issue, one must ask "why?" three times. If the answer to any one of those "whys" is, "because that's the way we've always done it," you know you're in trouble. We should do everything with specific purpose and godly determination. Every method of every programme of every church has a sell-by date. There comes a time to come back to the drawing board and change what doesn't work. I go to many churches and ask myself, "Why did they do that?" In some places, the announcements are at the beginning of the service when only half of the people are there. Sometimes there is an unnecessary gap between every song when there could be a seamless link so as to ensure the congregation's continual focus in worship. Why? We often preach in a style that is technically brilliant and theologically noteworthy, but unless people are listening and can apply it to their lives, there is no point in preaching. The time has come to review and create fresh new ways of doing church.

Rick Warren from Saddleback Community Church has spent a lot of time rethinking the way we do church. In doing so his book, *The Purpose-Driven Church has* become a multi-million seller.[1] He likens church to a baseball pitch that takes people from the community to the crowd, from the crowd to the congregation, from the congregation to the committed and from the committed to the core. His style is relaxed and casual as he incorporates into church the new relational culture in which we are living in today. His methods are well organised and purpose-driven: it's a winning combination!

Winning ideas

Every year we rebuild our church and renew every pro-gramme and every person involved. We have developed a "change culture". Change is anticipated, not resisted. William Booth had the idea of taking the pub songs of his day and putting Christian lyrics to them and taking them onto the streets. A winning idea. I recently went to a small European conference and heard some more winning ideas. A young man in Iceland has created an open door into every school with his suicide prevention programme. When he introduces God into the equation, because of this young man's vital role, nobody dares complain! A young woman in Australia has started a national school prayer day, where, once a year, Christians amass in the school grounds and publicly pray for the school and the town. It's a winning idea. A young man from Norway has started hundreds of Christian clubs in schools, which are run by the kids themselves. Maybe some of your new ideas are worth more than a penny. You may not see them in action around you, but they could be!

Maybe you have exciting ideas for making money for the kingdom of God. It might be as easy as it was for the guy who invented Velcro. Georges de Mestral decided to discover why flower burrs held on so well to items of clothing. He discovered that they had a tiny hook on the end – hey presto, a winning idea! It might be a gap in the market that you are to fill. Your ideas might take you into areas in which the gospel has never been preached. They might lead you to people who are keys to the local area, like Aquila or the Ethiopian eunuch. Your ideas might establish a business that makes millions for the kingdom of God.

Start thinking. Your thoughts are worth millions if they result in the kingdom of God being extended on the earth. It's time for the entrepreneurial spirit to arise!

BECOME AN ISLAND

"Hey. Man Friday! Come and see what's been washed up today!"

They say no man is an island. God must love islands, as He created so many of them! Before God does anything great through any person He first takes them to an island to instruct, train and prepare them for greatness. An island is a place of obscurity and solitude, far from the madding crowd. Islands are often places we like to holiday upon. God's islands can be lonely places, places of intensity, where one is deprived of friendship and support.

When people rise to prominence in either the Christian or the secular scene, we often think of them as an overnight sensation. For most, nothing could be further from the truth. For years the Irish band The Corrs had all the flair they needed to get to the top. They looked great, sounded great and could actually play their own musical instruments! Their slow ballad *Runaway* was incredibly popular and it rose into many top-ten charts across the world. As the masses stepped into the music stores, little did they realise that this particular single had already been released three times previously. Each of the other attempts to break into the marketplace had failed. The Corrs were not instant successes. Elton John did not seem to exist 40 years ago and yet he is well into his fifties. Nobody knew the young Reg Dwight as he sat in obscurity and began to write the songs that would take the world by storm. Darlene Zschech has become one of the greatest worship leaders and songwriters of our time. She emerged internationally with the song "Shout to the Lord". Only a few people have seen her years of penning songs that no one sang, together with the sowing of her life into her local church.

The beauty of obscurity

Moses had 40 years of obscurity. He emerged as one of the Old Testament's greatest leaders. David had thirteen years. Paul had a decade of obscurity in his hometown of Tarsus before being found by Barnabas and taken to Antioch. Jesus had 30 years of obscurity dressed (up) as a carpenter, waiting for the mission to begin.

God cannot be known naturally. You can see Him reflected through people, actions and words, but it takes revelation to know Him. That's why Paul prayed for the Ephesians that God would "enlighten the eyes of their understanding" (Ephesians 1:18). Often, to get real revelation, God has to take you out of your normal world, and lead you onto an island –

a place of isolation. You find yourself without your usual means of support. The friends you once relied upon are now gone. The money that you saved for a rainy day is now spent. The family that was so supportive is now opposed to you. You wonder what's going on – God is taking you to His island. It starts off as a desert and, as you spend time in His presence, it becomes a paradise. It was in the desert that Moses got the vision and the commission to rescue the Hebrew slaves. It was while running from Saul, sleeping in caves and crevices, that David broke into a world of revelation – so much so that his Psalms provide windows into a world thick with God. Revelation has nothing to do with circumstance; it is independent of whether you've had a bad father or a good father. A lot of people make excuses for not knowing God as well as they'd like to. They blame their history for their lack of knowledge of God. But revelation and faith are from another world entirely.

Between a rock and a hard place

I have known many times when I've felt that I was between a rock and a hard place. Nobody understood my efforts and no one came to my rescue. I thank God now for each of those times. He has been my rescuer, and my greatest messages have stemmed from my island experiences. I've had a revelation that He is my defender. It came from defenceless times. I have had a revelation that He is my rewarder. It came from thankless times. Revelation is everything. God truly builds His church upon it (Matthew 16:13–19).

It is in the hardest times that God reveals His greatest secrets. It is impossible to get a formula to open up the secrets of God, but people who want to know not only the hand of God, but also the heart of God, find them. Sometimes I sense nothing from heaven, but then light comes flooding into my soul, causing my heart to be changed. One thing I know is that if He is taking you to an island, then He is preparing a banquet for you. In the midst of your enemies and in the midst of adversity, He has a banquet waiting for you. There is a feast to be had, filled with the delicacies of heaven.

Islands become nations

Many times islands become nations. Somebody gets a fresh revelation and people flock to the island. Before long, what was born out of obscurity becomes front-page news and God launches you into prominence, sometimes overnight. Tommy Tenny had a revelation in the midst of a season of intimidation that it's not how talented you are but how *hungry* you are that counts for God. His revelation, born on an island, has become a ministry of international significance. Bill Hybels had a revelation that people matter to God. His Willow Creek Church has grown to become America's largest as God has taken His revelation to the masses. When you see people flocking to a fresh move of God, somebody somewhere dug a well and found the hidden waters of God.

Are you being taken to an island? It may look dark and lonely, but God is there! He is there ready with His tables of choice foods. He is ready to bless. Count it a privilege that God has chosen you to find the hidden manna. Get filled and sorted with God, because there comes a time when what happened in secret will one day be openly rewarded (Matthew 6:6). Your island may indeed become a nation. There may be a generation of seekers who, like you, God has separated out to prepare the way for a national revival. One day your islands will unite to form a continent of power, an unstoppable force for the kingdom of God.

SQ #18
BE TOO BIG FOR YOUR BOOTS

"I blame it on the rise in street theatre"

They say, "You're too big for your boots." You ought to be either too big or too small, but never just right. The thing about boots on children is that they never quite fit. If they are a new pair, they have been bought with room to grow. If they are an old pair, the toes are almost poking out of the end. Clothes are the same. Every smart mother dresses her eight-year-old in clothes that fit a nine-year-old. They might look a little funny, but it is smart thinking.

Growth is natural. Stunted growth is abnormal. Peter's second book encourages us to be committed to an increasing measure (2 Peter 1:8). He encourages us to add to our faith a whole package of things: goodness, wisdom, self-control, stickability, godliness, kindness and love. He then promises that if you possess each of these things in increasing measure, you'll be incredibly productive for the kingdom of God.

Many things in life come along to stunt our growth. Maybe your building is too small for your church. Maybe it's just right and everybody is quite comfortable. It's time to find a bigger venue and allow people to grow into it. Maybe financially, life has become quite comfortable for you. It's time to enlarge your vision and stretch yourself beyond human possibility. Maybe your job has become tight and you feel claustrophobic. It may be time for a new challenge and for you to step into a bigger world. I remember finally reaching the top of primary school. It took a while to get there and I was finally king of the castle. What a rude shock I got when I entered secondary school. I was now back to being bottom of the pile. Unless I'd made the transition (not that it was an option), I never would have made it to university and I would still be at primary school. Here are a few ways to take off the things that stunt your growth and put you into bigger boots for a bigger day.

Hang around big people

They say, "Pick on someone your own size." I say pick on someone much bigger than you. Many of us hang around with the people who are on the same level as we are or who aren't doing as well. The key to becoming big is to hang around people who stretch you, confront you and have the capacity to intimidate you. There are people who are much bigger than you are. Some of my biggest breakthroughs have come by associating with people who seem to be having much more success than I have ever had. I have had to fight intimidation and replace it with inspiration.

I remember being challenged to give financially to someone who was doing much better than I was when it came to money. In fact his house was worth millions. I didn't want to be stunted by a poverty spirit. I didn't want to give the "old man" in me any chance of a comeback. I wanted to be added to in increasing measure. One day I visited his house and slipped some money behind the telephone, to be found later. The money would have meant nothing to him, but for me it was a key to a bigger heart.

Possess super-vision

Vision is not enough. You need "super-vision". A supervisor is someone who is responsible for every procedure on the shop floor. If they're selling socks, he's responsible for the sock stocks and the quantity of socks produced (they must be even numbers!). He is responsible for the quality of workmanship as well as for the welfare of the stock workers. That's "super-vision". I've seen some people excel in family life, yet they are so sloppy in church life. I have seen some ministers be brilliant at pulpit-dynamics, but not good at people-dynamics. Some lose their spouses simply through a lack of "super-vision". They say that it's not the sand in a man's shoe that holds back a desert traveller, but one grain of sand in the eye. Marathon runners can do all the preparation preceding the 26-mile race, but if they don't tie their shoelaces they're in trouble!

Is there anything that you're neglecting in your life? I've told a few people that they need to lose weight if they're to succeed in the long term. It takes only one weak link to break the chains of endeavour.

Be a brain surgeon later on

A lot of Christians want to be a brain surgeon before they are a general practitioner. One thing they wouldn't let me do at school was to learn just a few subjects. I hated some of the subjects that I did and saw them as just excess baggage. Today it is some of those subjects that have helped me most in my life. Colin Dye, leader of the largest Pentecostal church in Britain, said that once he finds out a person's strengths and leanings (possibly through doing a personality and gift-ings profile) he finds a job that requires none of them. Why? He is committed to creating ambidextrous people, people strong in both the left arm and the right. He is committed to making GPs. We box ourselves off too early with hidden gifts and talents in each one of us that continue to lie dormant for years.

> *It takes only one weak link to break the chains of endeavour*

Often there's a certain prestige that comes from being a specialist. Resist it. Some would love to preach. Others would love to be prophets. Whilst we need to be released into our ministry giftings, we also need to realise that living a 24/7 Christian lifestyle requires us to be everything from an evangelist to a seat-putter-outer for the sake of the people in the world that God wants us to influence. I would see myself as a generalist, not a specialist. I preach, but it's only for a few hours each week. I declare God's directional word but it's only from time to time. I'm hooked on all aspects of church life. I want to see every person succeed. We all have certain strengths that we develop and maximise over time, but we all need to learn the basics before specialising in the specifics.

Talk to strangers

Familiarity breeds contentment! If you're always doing the same thing and always travelling on the same path, you'll attract the disease of contentment. You'll grow stagnant. It's time to stretch your wings and meet new people and experience new things. They say, "Don't talk to strangers," but I say that every new idea and friend starts as a stranger! Every future associate starts off as a stranger. Some hide away and expect the answers to prayers to come right into their living room. Many answers are out there – they're strangers ready to be met.

If your boots fit, throw them away and get a bigger pair. Get rid of all the restrictions that could hold back the dynamic growth that God has in store for your life and ministry. It was in the 1950s that Edmund Hillary attempted to climb Everest. He tried three times and failed. He finally succeeded when he joined a British expedition and was in the strongest position to be the first to reach the top with Sherpa Tensing. After his three attempts, he once looked at a picture of Everest and said, "You can't get any bigger, but we can!" It was that spirit that conquered the highest mountain in the world. He was prepared to grow into a new set of boots. Come on – let's take that spirit and expand our future horizons.

KICK A MAN WHEN HE'S DOWN

"Nice comic timing, Coco."

They say, "Don't kick a man when he's down." That is *exactly* when to kick. The wisdom of life is to know both what and when to attack. Somebody once said that if you're in a field of tigers and you're chasing rabbits, you need to watch out for the tigers. If you're in a field of rabbits and you're chasing tigers, you don't need to worry about the rabbits. Life is about knowing what to chase and what to avoid. Every day, I'm enticed into many boxing rings. I have to learn that distraction is one of Satan's major devices and I'm not falling for it. Like the rabbits and the tigers, I want to pick my fights. I don't want them to pick me!

After choosing the right battles, the next challenge is to know when to punch – when to take authority over satanic

strategies. Muhammad Ali, who was called the human butterfly, became the world heavyweight champion because he
knew when to strike. He was both a shadow boxer and a
knockout boxer. He learned the art of exhausting his oppo-
nent and then stepping in for the kill. The Bible says that
anyone who desires to live a godly life will face persecution
(2 Timothy 3:12). All those with desires to expand their
borders will experience opposition. The Promised Land
doesn't just need inhabiting, it needs invading. Here are some
keys to help you pack your punch and give you a convincing
kick.

Be confident that the battle belongs to God

It's not your fight; it's the Lord's. Stop taking it personally.
It's not you who is being resisted; it is the Lord. Joshua was
hyped up and ready to roll. The time had come for him to
strut his stuff. When Joshua moved closer to Jericho, he saw
an angel with a sword drawn in his hand. Joshua blurted
out, "Are you for us or against us?" The angel said,
"Neither." Joshua fell down and worshipped as he recognised the presence of the Lord (Joshua 5:13–15). The Lord
wasn't for Joshua; Joshua was for the Lord. The Lord was not
fighting for Joshua; Joshua was fighting for the cause of the
Lord. God does not fight our battles; we fight *His* battles. I
once had an incredible battle going on in my mind. I've got
traces of what psychologists call ADD: Attention Deficiency
Disorder. It is the paradoxical condition of having an inability to concentrate for long lengths of time, together with an
incredible ability to super-concentrate for short periods of
time. For some, this results in hyperactivity. The calming

drug Ritalin is used by over 2 million children in the US every day to combat it. My hyperactivity is largely internalised and results in a mind that is always busy and always switched on, even if it is a screen saver! I'm prone to obsessions and fixations. One day, in my mid-twenties, I became obsessively self-conscious about my mouth both when I was talking to people and even when I was on my own. I prayed and tried to fight it, but it would not shift. Eventually, I took hold of the scriptural truth that the battle belonged to the Lord. Every time the fixation surfaced, I simply said to myself that this battle did not belong to me but to the Lord. He did not want me to fight this battle. The strategy that God gave me worked and the thoughts that plagued me were now kept at bay.

Be confident in the hornets

In the book of Exodus, God said, "I will send the hornet ahead of you to drive the Hivites, Canaanites and Hittites out of your way" (Exodus 23:28). The hornets were there to sting the enemy and to place him in a weakened state. For the inhabitants of Canaan, God sent great terror on the land and all peoples trembled with fear (Joshua 2:9). Sometimes He sends the enemy into confusion (Judges 7:22). Sometimes He causes the enemy to forget to dress for war (2 Kings 3). All of Israel's battles that God directed were easier to win than they ought to have been. Many battles were in the enemy's favour but they fell to the Israelites. Why? God had weakened

Charles Spurgeon once wrote, "The air is full of mysterious influences, which harass Israel's foes"

them. He'd sent in the hornets. He got the Israelites to punch and kick when the enemy was down. That's strategy! Charles Spurgeon once wrote, "The air is full of mysterious influences, which harass Israel's foes."[1] Be confident that, right now, the stinging hornets sent by God are attacking any resistance to your advancement. An unseen adversary, God himself, is attacking the devil's strategies and devices. God is exercising His authority, even though you cannot see it.

Be confident in the sound of the trumpet

Before the fall of Jericho, the priests blew the trumpets and the people gave up a great shout (Joshua 6:20). Before Gideon won the battle against the hordes of Midianites, they blew their trumpets and held up their torches (Judges 7:20). Jehoshaphat sang praises (2 Chronicles 20:22). There's a time to declare the purposes of God to both people and spiritual principalities. Never underestimate the power of the prophetic punch. When the time is right, you need to shout. You'll know about that time when you sense His authority and His unction coming upon you. If it's habits in your life that have grown to plague you, let the liberating prophetic shout dismiss them out of hand. If it's the spirit of rebellion or the spirit of poverty that is seeking to disrupt your advancement, let the prophetic shout knock them to the ground.

Never underestimate the power of the prophetic punch

Many times as a church we exercise the power of the shout. Almost every Sunday service, we declare the truth of victory and wield the sword of the Spirit, and we give up a shout! We do it over our own personal lives, over our families, our church and our city. Many times it has resulted in a dramatic turnaround.

After spending all of our money on building renovation, my team and I found the church budget contained very little money to pay the wages of our staff the following week. On the Saturday night after completing the renovations, I felt a nudge from God to give away all of Sunday's offerings and trust Him for all of our needs. I told it to my team, and all of us were in agreement that it was the right thing to do. We gave the entire and much-needed offering to the local community. It was the largest offering we had ever taken – I was tempted to keep it! We gave a few hundred pounds to the schools in the local area, and even gave fifty pounds to the local pub. The shop on the nearby estate still has our fifty pounds: they're finding it hard to spend because they seem to think it is holy money! God has never let us down from that point on. Our giving was a prophetic declaration that God was our financial supplier and that our bank was the bank of heaven.

Warfare is always strategic. Remember to get God's plan of attack each time you invade! Make sure you give God's hornets time to weaken your enemy and declare God's promises and His praises. He promises us the victory when we walk in His ways. There's a time to take authority over your enemy. Think about it: it could be right now.

"110% of nothing is still nothing, Oliver"

They say, "This time I want you to give 110%." Impossible! The maximum effort you can make is 100%. Full stop. The idea of giving 110% is doomed to failure because it simply isn't possible. Even with the power of the resurrection behind you, it's still an impossibility. If you have goals that you consistently fail to attain, discouragement will cause you to give much less than 100%. To give 100% is to give everything, no holds barred. When a certain lawyer asked Jesus what he had to do to inherit eternal life, Jesus replied, "Love the Lord your God with all your heart and with all your soul and with all your strength and with all your mind," and, "Love your neighbour as yourself" (Luke 10:27).

Jesus outlined the four parts to your being that require 100% devotion.

Your heart represents your convictions, and your mind represents your commitments. Your soul represents your character, and your strength represents both your confession and your conduct. When your convictions, commitments, character, confession and conduct each reach 100% devotion towards the cause of Jesus Christ, almost anything could happen. Many people have good convictions but still live their lives outside (of) them. What you *think* about what God has said about you and what God has actually said are sometimes two different things. What you say is often nothing like what you really believe. Unity doesn't begin with two people, but with one person. When all of your inner man comes into line with your God-centred convictions, unity is established and God begins to command a blessing (Psalm 133). Watch out!

The death zone

David's army consisted of twelve divisions, each consisting of 12,000 men. In 2 Samuel 23, 42 men are listed as being very special. Out of these, eight are singled out for greater commendation. Out of the eight, five dared to go it alone. They dared to stand in the death zone and risk all for the cause of the kingdom. Josheb-Basshebeth stood single-handedly against 800 men. He slew every one of them. Eleazar gave 100% of his heart, soul, strength and mind – his hand froze to the sword he was holding. Shammah gave his all for a field of lentils. He treated it like a field full of gold! A sense of duty will never get you into the death zone. It is only true love that causes someone to excel into excess and become a 100%er. To conquer Everests, win wars and gain access to the intimate secrets of God takes more than duty – it takes a person who is truly, madly, deeply in love. All of David's men who are listed in the Bible come under the generic title "David's mighty men". Even though it's about the might of God, the credit still goes to the sanctified might of the man. Often we will wait around for a move of the Spirit, yet God is simply waiting for a move of the man! Until we give our best, He won't release His best. God moves in after we move into the thick of the battle.

> *Often we will wait around for a move of the Spirit, yet God is simply waiting for a move of the man!*

Surprise! Surprise!

We wait for God to lead and speak to us about too many things. When it comes to offerings, we're encouraged to ask the Holy Spirit to see how much He wants us to give. Sometimes He complies. To consistently ask the Holy Spirit is to risk missing out on the essence of love – the element of surprise. If I asked my wife what she wanted for Christmas and then told her what I'd got, she'd be pleased but not ecstatic. She's only over the moon when I've kept the element of surprise and she's awoken to a gift for which I have added my initiative to her guidance. Sometimes the giving of gifts can fall into something resembling a business transaction rather than into the unpredictable realm of love where excess is legendary. I once encouraged our congregation to do some alabaster-jar giving in order to raise a large offering. Everybody has an alabaster jar in their lives. It might be some treasure kept for a rainy day. It might be something kept for a very special day. For the woman who broke her alabaster jar and poured its precious contents over Jesus, it was something of incredible worth that she had been keeping for her wedding day (Matthew 26:6–7). Whatever the case – it's costly and personal and it's an offering way beyond the call of duty. Never does the scripture indicate that the Holy Spirit asked the woman to crack open the jar and pour out its contents. She initiated it. Love compelled her. It was for Jesus, an awesome act of worship. For our offering, I encouraged people *not* to ask the Holy Spirit how much to give! This was to be a surprise for God. It was to be self-initiated and something that God would remember fondly as He thought through the history of Hope City Church. We took up a phenomenal offering. In quantity it was good, but in quality it was outstanding. I'm sure it knocked God's socks off. People went far beyond the call of duty and entered into an arena that belongs to the excessive – those who are madly in love with Jesus. They didn't give 110%, they gave 100% and, like the praise Jesus gave to the woman who broke her jar, God gave 100% of His attention to it.

Sleepless in Seattle

I remember hearing about the romantic exploits of Phil Wagner, Pastor of Oasis Christian Center in Los Angeles. One day he disappeared and left a note for his wife, Holly, to get ready for a very special trip. He told her to pack for four days and he'd meet her in New York. After a flight across America, she found herself getting chauffeur-driven to the Empire State building. At the top, Phil was waiting for her entrance. She was blown out because it was just like a scene in her favourite movie, *Sleepless in Seattle*. Phil had initiated a superb idea, and she was the recipient. It was true love rekindled![1]

One of Britain's favourite shows on television is called *Changing Rooms*. The idea is that neighbours swap houses for a couple of days and each pair renovates a specific room in the other couple's house. With the help of an eccentric interior designer, they're each allowed to spend up to five hundred pounds. It's not a lot of money, but often when the owner comes back, and is allowed to see the results, tears are not far away. You can give someone five hundred pounds and they'd say, "Thanks!" But convert that five hundred pounds into time, effort, thought and attention and you'll not only get thanks, you'll also touch deep into a human heart.

What a blast God gets when He receives your gifts of love and your devotion of heart, mind, soul and strength toward His plans. Those who enter into this realm are liable to receive much more from God than could ever be anticipated. When faith and love meet, God breathes in the incense of true worship, and proceeds to breathe out the blessing of pure glory!

Forget the 110% giving. That's a recipe for demotivation – because you will constantly be frustrated. Aim to give all of what you have. Give 100%. Step into the area of devotion reserved for those head-over-heels in love. Passion will take you into the death zone where the duty-bound fear to tread. Love will take you to summits that give you views which penetrate the depths of vision and revelation that the gates of hell will never be able to prevail against.

JUDGE BOOKS BY THEIR COVERS

"Do you think we could ask Uncle Albert to stop sending these magazines for Sidney?"

They say, "Don't judge a book by its cover." I say, judge it. Within you are both a natural capacity and a spiritual capacity to make sound judgements, after looking at all the evidence.

Jesus said that a lot can be deduced from searching through the evidence. He said that "every good tree bears good fruit, but a bad tree bears bad fruit" (Matthew 7:17). Good fruit means good root – bad fruit means bad root.

Many Christians are too open-minded. Sometimes it's to counteract the thought of being too closed-minded! Being closed-minded or "dogmatic" is to fail to do a thorough search of the facts. Not being opinionated doesn't mean that you should not have an opinion! Often, we regard the thoughts of others so highly that we inadvertently devalue our own thoughts. For the maturing Christian, our thinking is being transformed and fashioned by the thinking of Christ. So much so that Paul said to the Corinthian Church, "But we have the mind of Christ" (1 Corinthians 2:16).

A crisis of confidence

I was surprised to find out that there are companies whose job it is to scan every newspaper and magazine on the market in order to clip out articles on particular stars. These famous personalities actually *pay* these companies in order to find out what everybody is saying. Why do stars care so much about what the critics are saying about them? Surely they don't represent the opinions of all the population? Well, sadly, they often do. Although they don't really reflect the original views of the audience, they tend actually to create their views. So much of society is so unsure about their own opinions that they simply take the perspective of the critic and regurgitate it to everyone in the office block! So many lack the confidence to disagree. It was the critique of the press that determined mass opinion on Europe's greatest tourist attraction of the millennium – the Millennium Dome. Even though it had more visitors than any other tourist attraction in the whole of Europe in the year 2000, the British papers wrote the Dome off. People then followed the critics. If they happened to enjoy the Millennium Dome experience, they kept it very quiet!

Often, Christians keep their opinions and thoughts quiet and only handle "second-hand" thoughts. In many churches where a presentation has been made on a Sunday morning, the congregation looks to the minister to see what they all thought of it! This reveals a mixture of both respect and lack of confidence in their own judgements and thoughts.

Stripped bare

I remember when my wife once opened my briefcase and saw a pile of books and magazines inside. She asked me what I was doing with it all. I told her that I needed it for my sermon. Some contained great stories, others great spiritual insights! She saw that I also had with me about three different versions of the Bible. After challenging me as to why I needed so many varieties of scripture and so much reading material, she began to take it all away and place it in a nearby cupboard. I was left with just one Bible. I cried for hours! You see, my confidence wasn't in what *I* thought, but in what others thought. My ideas on God and his word and the journey of life that I had led had been downgraded and replaced with everybody else's thoughts. From that moment on, it was back to just me and God's word. What a difference that would eventually make to my life. From being a young boy, my opinions were constantly overshadowed by the right opinions of others. I grew up without the confidence-building affirmation that one needs to believe in oneself. As I began to realise that as a Christian I was developing "the mind of Christ", I knew that many of my thoughts had to be as valuable as the thoughts of others. Even people with very large churches!

Ever-increasing confidence

When God speaks to us it creates faith right in the very heart of us (Romans 10:17). That kind of impartation of faith gives us a flash of confidence and a feeling of excitement that God is about to break through. The confidence that carries us through, though, isn't that initial confidence that is directly linked to what God has just said to us. We can have great faith but little continuing confidence. We can have faith yet continue to live in the land of doubt, oscillating between what God has said and what someone else once said, or what the devil has whispered in our ear. Confidence is all to do with what we think about what God has said. When you start to value the thoughts that initially radiated out of the revelation and fresh encounter you had with God, you'll start to develop ever-increasing confidence. The more we agree with what God has said to us, the more we create an ever-increasing river bed within our minds that will eventually seem natural for our stream of consciousness to flow down.

Sometimes when God speaks to me, I hold it in my heart for a while, not even telling my beautiful wife. I may have heard from God, but I still lack the channelled-out river beds of new thinking that need to accompany such lofty new thoughts from God. Sharing too early with an unexcitable audience can trigger us into devaluing the revelation and dismissing our new-found thinking process. Sometimes it's wise to hang on to your pearl before you cast it to the fields.

True leadership

Leadership is all about making right and responsible decisions. They say that the way to tell a leader from someone who is not is to take them to an Indian restaurant and ask them to choose from the menu. The length of time it takes them to choose will reveal the degree of leadership within the person. A decision made too quickly might give away an underlying impulsiveness and result in them having to digest the most toxic vindaloo known to the Western world. Too slow a decision can betray an underlying indecisiveness and prevent the rest of the table from satisfying their appetites. Many decisions are not cut and dried. Some decisions have 51% in favour and 49% against. A person who has developed confidence goes with the 51% as if it is 100%. They "commit"! After making a wise choice, they come out from the shadow of doubt and fly their colours. That's the hallmark of true leadership.

Clouded judgement

It's important, when making decisions about your future and the future of others, not to allow any personal issues to cloud your judgement. A critical spirit and unforgiveness can cause us to lose our perspective and make a series of "wrong calls". Samuel had a personal concern when selecting a king who would replace Saul. Samuel's idea of a king was that he should have "the look" that stood head and shoulders above the rest. Upon seeing Jesse's first son, he thought that he'd found the next king. Eliab looked great! God had to readjust Samuel's way of thinking, which was affecting his discernment. The Lord said, "Man looks at the outward appearance, but the LORD looks at the heart" (1 Samuel 16:7). Samuel had to dismiss his own bias.

He who walks with the wise grows wise, but a companion of fools suffers harm

Lastly, it's important that you seriously consider the wise advice of Christians in leadership. The Bible tells us, "He who walks with the wise grows wise, but a companion of fools suffers harm" (Proverbs 13:20). As you inspect the evidence and gather the important opinions of wise people, it is then time to fashion your own opinion and make the necessary decisions that result from it.

Loveable rogues

There are some people who have been classified as "loveable rogues". We say that they have a good heart and mean well, but they exhibit signs of recklessness and unfaithfulness. We constantly give them another chance and sway heavily towards letting them off the hook. They have a knack of twisting people around their little finger! There is no such thing as a "loveable rogue". Jesus is clear – a bad tree bears bad fruit. The fruit is evidence that their heart is bad, not good. They don't just need forgiveness, they also need a change of heart. You might like them, but to truly love them requires both grace and discipline.

It is time to trust your judgements. If you've inspected the fruit and listened to the opinions of trusted people, you can make a good judgement as to what decisions to take. You simply need to exercise the power of observation, use the discernment of the Spirit (as in the case of Samuel selecting Jesse's eighth son and not his first), and have the confidence of your renewed thinking patterns. Hebrews 10:35 encourages us never to throw away our confidence because one day it will be richly rewarded. Your thoughts count!

Epilogue

DON'T CUT TO THE CHASE

Principally, life isn't about chasing as much as it is about walking. It's more of a marathon than a sprint. One of the great days in the life of a parent is when their young child walks for the first time unaided. Walking is an art, not just a function. It requires that all of our weight shift from one leg to the other and back again until we reach our destination. We remain balanced, although our weight distribution is not.

In understanding the art of walking, we can boost our SQ – our spiritual intelligence. We can be a Calvinist one week and an Armenian the next! We can be buying up houses and land one month and giving it away the next. We can be both tough

> *It is only as you piece together his truths that you start to see the whole picture of the way Jesus walked*

and tender, reflective and outrageous. Intelligent living has an ability to shift from one emphasis to a seemingly opposing emphasis, while remaining balanced and upright. Some have made balance a law of averages that keeps a person in conservatism. This conservatism is reflected in 21 of the world's most popular sayings. They constantly counterbalance their beliefs with checks and balances and end up merely standing around doing very little and being very average. Jesus was the opposite. He constantly taught extremes and caught imaginations with penetrating truths. It is only as you piece together His truths that you start to see the whole picture of the way Jesus walked.

I love extremes. At home I'm either extremely tidy or extremely messy. There is a difference, though, between walking in extremes and lurching in them. Many churches lurch from side to side as they chase after new fads and "lucky" teachings. The dangers of tripping abound. As they stay on one foot too long they soon start to lose their sense of

> *Spiritual intelligence is not only about breaking conservatism, but also about "ever increasing"*

balance. A walker moves swiftly from one foot to the other. The outcome is the ability to balance extremes, which produces a pattern of sound teaching, not just a thread of it.

As we have seen, spiritual intelligence is not only about breaking conservatism, but also about "ever increasing". As we grow in Christ, our stride increases and new territory is gained. Peter challenges us to have an "increasing measure" (2 Peter 1:8). The Christian life is a journey of growth. Our capacity, our ability and our faith are growing as we move into our God-given destiny. I trust that this book has assisted you in your growth and added strategies to your life that will help harness mind, soul, strength and heart for the cause of the kingdom.

My prayer is that you never become a one-hit wonder but that you may have hit after hit after hit. Rise up and be legends in the land!

NOTES

SQ #1

1 Phil Baker is the leader of Riverview Church in Perth, Western Australia. He heads up the "Australian Christian Churches" and runs church network conferences in Australia and Europe.

2 John C. Maxwell, *Developing the Leader Within You* (Word Publishing, 1993) p. 136

3 Konrad Adenauer (Source unknown)

SQ #2

1 Will Carling and Robert Heller, *The Way to Win* (Warner Books, 1995) Chapter 4

2 Steve Kennedy, Pastor of Liberty Church, Logan City, Queensland, Australia

SQ #3

1 Andrew Oliver, European Leadership Consultation with Mal Fletcher, Copenhagen, April 2001

SQ #5

1 Dick Innes, "Failure: Never Forever" *Encounter Magazine* (reprint, Acts International Publishing)

SQ #6

1 *Vanity Fair* (November 1997) p. 207
2 Oswald J. Smith "Mission Pioneering" Source unknown.

SQ #7

1 Roger Steer, *George Müller – Delighted in God* (Harold Shaw Publishers, 1985) p. 161

SQ #10

1 Margaret Atkins, "Faith and Reason", *The Independent* (24th February 2001)

SQ #11

1 Richard Branson, *Losing my Virginity* (Virgin Publishing, 1999)
2 Chris Bonington, Article *Night and Day* magazine (*Daily Mail*, 21st January 2001)

SQ #13

1 Jenny Cooney Corillo, "He shoots, He scores" *High Life* magazine (British Airways) p. 68

SQ #16

1 Rick Warren, *The Purpose-Driven Church* (Zondervan Publishing, 1995)

SQ #19

1 C.H. Spurgeon, *Faith's Checkbook* (Moody Press) p. 48

SQ #20

1 Holly Wagner, *Dumb Things She Does – Dumb Things He Does* (*Wine Press* Publishing, 1999) p. 42